CW01369162

Royal Botanic Gardens Kew

THE KEW GARDENER'S GUIDE TO

GROWING HERBS

Royal Botanic Gardens Kew

THE KEW GARDENER'S GUIDE TO

GROWING HERBS

THE ART AND SCIENCE TO
GROW YOUR OWN HERBS

HOLLY FARRELL

WHITE LION PUBLISHING

Contents

6   INTRODUCTION TO GROWING HERBS

22 PLANTS

24 English mace
25 Electric daisy
26 Anise hyssop
27 Chives

28 PROJECT 1: A VERTICAL HERB GARDEN

30 Garlic chives
31 Wild garlic
32 Lemon verbena
33 Dill
34 Angelica
35 Chervil
36 Celery leaf
37 Horseradish
38 French tarragon
39 Orach

40 PROJECT 2: HERB OILS, VINEGARS, SPIRITS AND WATERS

42 Good King Henry
43 Borage
44 Mustard
45 Marigold
46 Carolina allspice
47 Chilli pepper
51 Caraway
52 Camomile
53 Chicory

54 PROJECT 3: HERBS AS CUT FLOWERS

56 Citrus bergamot
57 Lesser calamint
58 Coriander
59 Saffron

60 PROJECT 4: HERBAL TISANES

62 Cumin
63 Turmeric
64 Lemongrass
65 Epazote
66 Cardamom
67 Wasabi

68 PROJECT 5: HARVESTING SEED AND FENNEL POLLEN

70 Fennel
71 Sweet woodruff
72 Hop
73 Hyssop
74 Bay
75 English lavender

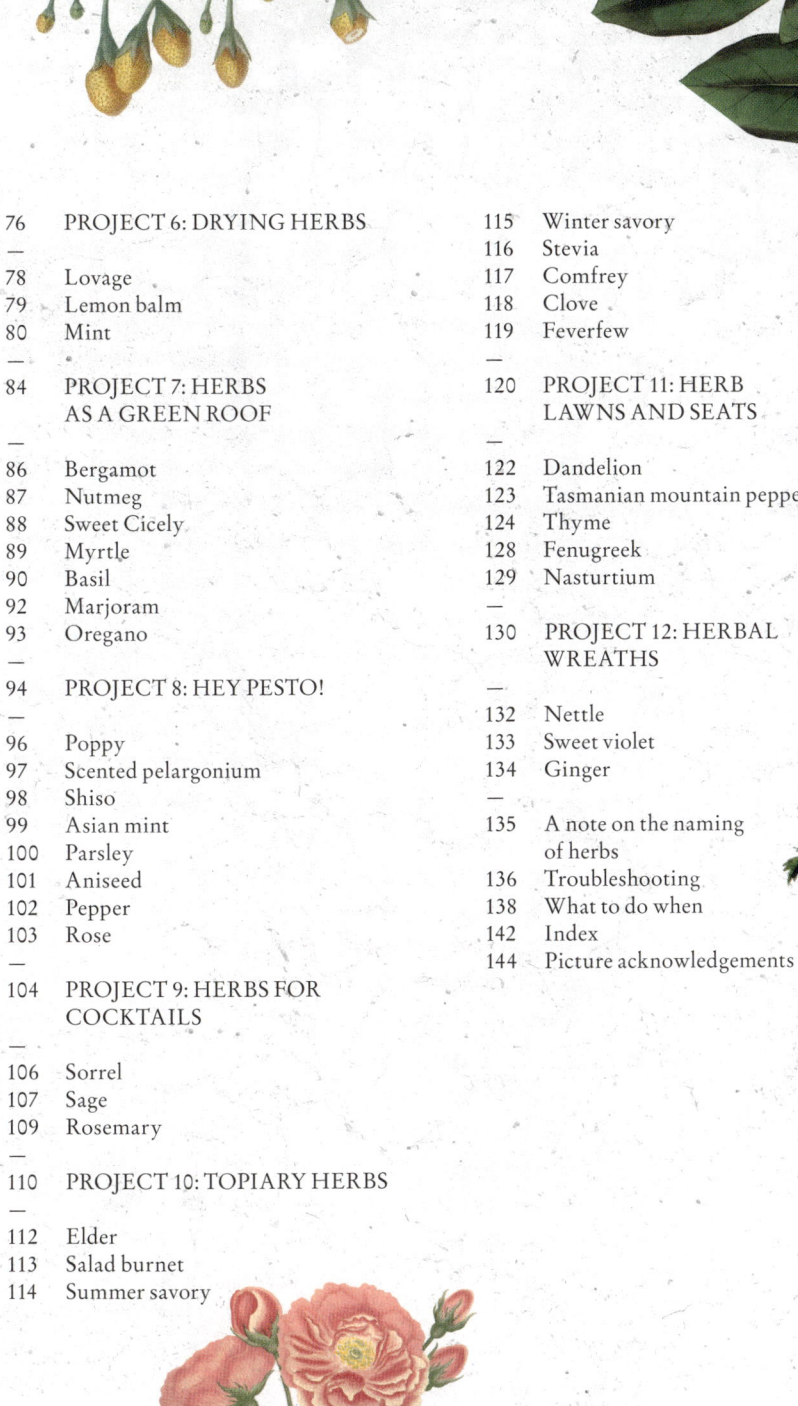

76	PROJECT 6: DRYING HERBS	115	Winter savory
		116	Stevia
78	Lovage	117	Comfrey
79	Lemon balm	118	Clove
80	Mint	119	Feverfew
84	PROJECT 7: HERBS AS A GREEN ROOF	120	PROJECT 11: HERB LAWNS AND SEATS
86	Bergamot	122	Dandelion
87	Nutmeg	123	Tasmanian mountain pepper
88	Sweet Cicely	124	Thyme
89	Myrtle	128	Fenugreek
90	Basil	129	Nasturtium
92	Marjoram		
93	Oregano	130	PROJECT 12: HERBAL WREATHS
94	PROJECT 8: HEY PESTO!	132	Nettle
96	Poppy	133	Sweet violet
97	Scented pelargonium	134	Ginger
98	Shiso		
99	Asian mint	135	A note on the naming of herbs
100	Parsley	136	Troubleshooting
101	Aniseed	138	What to do when
102	Pepper	142	Index
103	Rose	144	Picture acknowledgements
104	PROJECT 9: HERBS FOR COCKTAILS		
106	Sorrel		
107	Sage		
109	Rosemary		
110	PROJECT 10: TOPIARY HERBS		
112	Elder		
113	Salad burnet		
114	Summer savory		

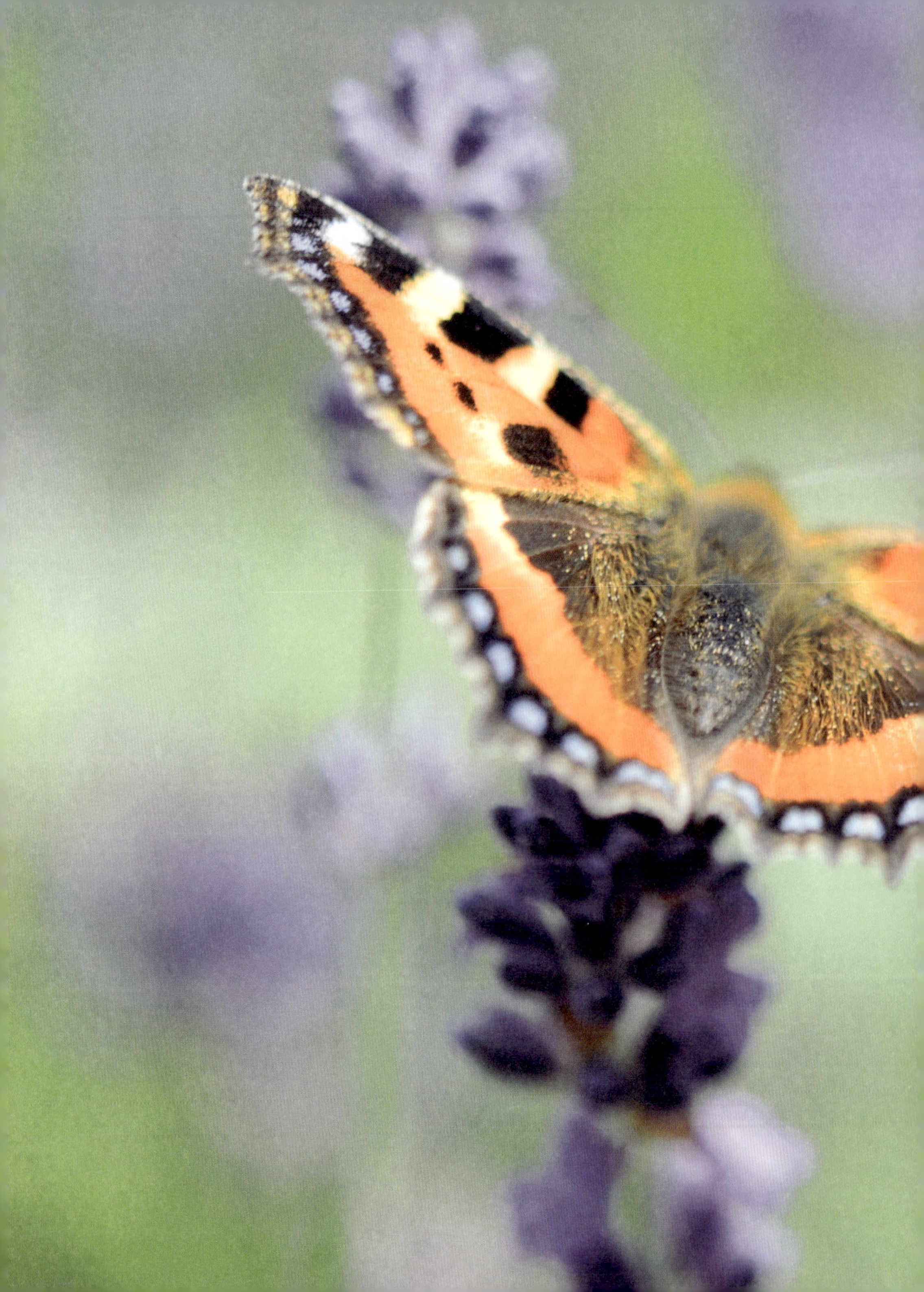

Introduction to growing herbs
—

INTRODUCTION

THE VALUE OF HERBS

The herbs in this book provide flavours and scents unlike any other: culinary herbs are a living trove of fresh flavours for any cook, with an almost alchemical power to transform the simplest dishes. Herbs can be used as seeds, flowers or leaves; be cooked and eaten; or be used to infuse a dish or drink. They are popping up in artisan gin, ice cubes and cocktail syrups and in foraged dishes and kitchen gardens of the best restaurants as chefs realize that often the only way to capture that elusive flavour is to have home-grown, freshly harvested herbs on their doorstep.

Since man's earliest forays into foraging and cultivating crops, herbs have been a vital part of our diet and economy. In addition to their myriad culinary applications, herbs have been used to dye cloth, heal the sick, perfume the body and home and even serve as money itself. Today, herbs form the basis (either naturally or chemically derived) of many medicines and remedies; are found in bouquets of cut flowers; are used in perfumes and dyes; and are invaluable plants for wildlife in the garden. In short, it is hard to think of a group of plants more useful to humankind than herbs – and this is the definition of herbs that has been as applied to plants in this book.

Botanically, a herb is a plant that has fleshy rather than woody stems (hence 'herbaceous'), but the range of plants that herbs include is far wider than that (although the more obvious food plants are excluded).

Many of the herbs historically used as medicine can be identified today using their Latin names – the species name *officinalis* denotes that it was once used by the apothecaries, but modern-day pharmaceutical companies rely on herbs perhaps more than they would care to admit. Most people are aware of the sedative powers of the opium poppy (still a main source of morphine) and perhaps have heard of quinine (from the bark of the genus *Cinchona*, which was the first discovered cure for malaria), but what about *Dioscorea*, which allowed the development of many steroids and oral contraceptive drugs?

Herbs are around us all the time, and many gardens will already include some of them whose uses are known to the gardener and others that are not: this book can enlighten and provide suggestions for plants to include. For those without gardens already, growing herbs can become an addictive process. Start with the basic introductory pack of the main culinary herbs (basil, thyme, mint, rosemary) but go beyond these, be adventurous, and try growing something new – herbs never disappoint.

HARDINESS ZONES

Each herb entry in this book has an associated hardiness zone rating. These ratings have been classified by the Royal Horticultural Society (RHS) to show how well a plant will grow in hot to freezing conditions. Plants in zones 1–2 will require frost-free conditions year-round; some will have even higher minimum temperatures. Plants that will survive a frost are in zones 3 and above, with higher zone numbers indicating a lower temperature below freezing that the plant will tolerate. Further details of the individual zones can be found on the RHS website (https://www.rhs.org.uk).

MUST-HAVE HERBS
Every garden – even if it is just a collection of pots on a windowsill – can make space for a herb or two. This book details more than seventy of the most popular, invaluable and most easily grown herbs. How to choose between them depends on how they are to be used.

Herbs provide colour and form: here purple sage contrasts with golden marjoram.

Herbs for cooks
Almost all herbs have some culinary application and there are many, many flavours to explore. These are a good starting point: rosemary, thyme, basil, chives, oregano, French tarragon, chillies, fennel, mint, parsley, sage, sorrel, savory, chicory and wild garlic.

Herbs for bakers
Among the most versatile are lemon verbena, thyme, rosemary, English

INTRODUCTION TO GROWING HERBS

INTRODUCTION

lavender, angelica, mint, fennel, saffron, bay, cardamom, Carolina allspice, sweet Cicely, scented pelargoniums, elderflower, rose, sweet violet and ginger.

Herbs for drinks
Whether it is for tea or a tipple, these herbs are all good to infuse or make drinks. Try mint, lemon verbena, thyme, fennel, camomile, lemon balm, rose and elder. See also Herbal tisanes, pages 60–1; and Herbs for cocktails, pages 104–105.

Herbs for crafters and florists
These flowers will all dry well, last as cut flowers or have a good scent: English mace, anise hyssop, lemon verbena, dill, lavender, bay, mint, rose, rosemary and feverfew. See also herbs as cut flowers, pages 54–5; and herbal wreaths, pages 130–31.

Herbs for wildlife
Almost all herbs are beloved by bees, butterflies and many other forms of garden wildlife: lavender, chives,

Chive flowers are beloved by bees of all stripes.

fennel, lesser calamint, marigold, mint, hyssop, oregano, lemon balm, rose, elder, sweet violet, nasturtium and nettle.

EASY-CARE HERBS
Growing plants is a fairly straightforward process – just give them light, water, nutrients and space to develop – but some species are more finicky than others and for the novice grower it is best to start with hardy, reliable plants. Fortunately, many herbs are dependable garden stalwarts, so there are plenty to choose from.

Tips for success
Choose a plant suitable for the growing conditions available to it. Ensure the plant is also appropriate for the climate – some herbs in this book are completely hardy, others are frost tender, and some need to be kept in warm conditions year-round. Humidity and light levels also need to be considered for some tropical plants.
    Start with just one or two plants and grow a herb garden gradually so new plants always follow successes rather than over-ambitious failures.

Easy herbs for a windowsill pot
Try thyme, chillies, basil, mint, parsley and scented pelargonium.

Easy herbs for a large pot outside
Choose mint, oregano, thyme, rosemary, lavender, bay, nasturtium, marigold, sweet violet, chives, lemon verbena or parsley.

Easy herbs to plant in the ground
Plant chives, rosemary, lavender, bay, oregano, nasturtium, marigold, sweet violet, borage, fennel, lemon balm, sage, elder, nettle, thyme and sorrel.

EQUIPMENT
Very few things are actually needed to start and maintain a herb garden. For tight budgets most things can be improvised at first from kitchen implements.

The essentials
- small watering can with a long, narrow spout, to reach the base of indoor plants;
- larger watering can with a rose, for outdoor plants;
- bypass secateurs;
- long-handled trowel;
- long-handled fork;
- spade;
- garden fork;
- rake;
- compost – for when planting in pots and as a mulch for garden beds and borders;
- fertilizers – controlled-release granules to mix with compost or liquids that can be diluted and watered on to the plants.

Useful extras
- hosepipe;
- hand saw;
- canes or other supports;
- soft horticultural twine/string;
- labels – for identifying seed sown or species in a herb garden;
- seed trays and small pots;
- heated propagator – for growing chillies;
- spray/misting bottle;
- gloves.

SOIL, SITUATION AND PREPARING THE GROUND
For new plants to flourish, they will need to be planted in their optimal site – a position to meet their soil, light level, shelter and temperature requirements. This is not to say a plant will not grow elsewhere, and to an extent one or other of these conditions can be stretched in order to accommodate it within a

Herbs can be grown in geometric patterns as well as lines.

Several herb plants can be accommodated in a single, large pot.

INTRODUCTION TO GROWING HERBS

INTRODUCTION

garden. Added protections such as horticultural fleece in winter can also be used to grow a less hardy plant in a colder spot than it prefers.

The main features of garden soil that pertain to the success of plants are its type and its drainage. Its pH – a measure of how acid or alkaline a soil is – can also affect growth but usually only when it is extreme (outside a range of pH6–7.5), and most gardens have a soil that is suitable for most plants. Soil type means whether a soil is primarily composed of clay, loam or sand. In general, clay soils tend to hold more water and nutrients than faster-draining, sandy soils, but they will crack open in dry weather and are slower to warm in spring. The ideal soil has a balance of all three soil types, with an additional good dose of organic matter (compost or well-rotted manure), which will keep a healthy balance in the soil ecosystem and maintain good water and nutrient levels. All soil can be improved with annual or twice-annual applications of organic matter as a mulch, which is then incorporated into the soil over the year by worms and other creatures.

The best soil and situation for a herb garden depends on the herbs to be planted. Mediterranean herbs need hot, sunny, free-draining positions for the most aromatic leaves (for example, rosemary, lavender and thyme); others prefer shade and moist soil (for example, mint, comfrey and wild garlic). Choose herbs that are most suitable for the garden's environment and consider planting other favourites in containers.

Preparing the ground for planting
Before planting a new area of ground, dig it over thoroughly to remove any weeds – including all their roots – and large stones, then cover it with a thick layer of well-rotted organic matter. Mix this into the soil using a garden fork and then shuffle over the area to consolidate (but not compact) it. Rake the soil level and smooth; it is then ready to plant. Lay out all the plants while still in their pots, so the design can be tweaked if necessary, then plant, raking out footprints at the end.

PERENNIAL HERBS
Perennials are plants that come back year on year. Even though they include shrubs and trees, which have woody stems, the term 'perennial' commonly refers to herbaceous (or non-woody) perennials and some subshrubs. Perennial herbs are some of the easiest to grow: they require little maintenance and are not subject to as many of the troubles that can affect the faster-growing, soft-stemmed annuals. They can be evergreen – retaining their leaves,

Wooden boxes are attractive and effective planters for herbs.

or most of their leaves, year-round, such as sweet violet; or be herbaceous – where the leaves and stems die back in autumn but the roots survive and sprout new shoots in spring. Herbaceous perennial herbs include mint, lemon balm, lovage, chives, fennel and sorrel.

Purchasing plants
When buying in garden centres, nurseries or other shops, always turn plants out of their pots to check the health of the roots, and that each plant is well established but not root-bound. Ensure the plant has healthy foliage, too. If you purchase while the plants are in growth, you will be able to check their health and plant identification, leaves can be sniffed for the best cultivar choice and so on. However, plants will usually be cheaper in winter.

Planting
Perennials are best planted in spring or autumn, when the soil is warm and moist. Prepare the ground and water well before planting. Make the planting hole wider but not deeper than the pot,

A small raised bed makes an excellent 'starter' herb patch.

turn the plant out of the pot and put it in the hole. Backfill around it, ensuring there is firm contact between the soil and the root ball, and water it in well.

Maintenance
Put in supports for tall plants – peasticks, wire rings, stakes – before they need them and tie in through the season if applicable. Most perennial herbs will benefit from being cut back after flowering (when they can get a little straggly) and will put on fresh foliage after this. Herbaceous perennials can have their old stems cut back in autumn (to prevent self-sowing) or in late winter (to provide winter food and shelter for wildlife).

SHRUBS AND TREES
Herbs that grow as shrubs and trees need not be limited to those with a large garden; some are perfectly happy in a large container, and as young plants many will even fit on a windowsill. Citrus, rosemary, lemon verbena, bay, lavender and myrtle are all examples of these. However, shrubs

Water all newly planted herbs well until they are fully established.

INTRODUCTION TO GROWING HERBS

INTRODUCTION

such as roses, elder and, in warmer climes, nutmeg must be planted in the ground or a large raised bed and given plenty of space. Climbers such as black pepper could be accommodated indoors – indeed in temperate climates many will need the extra heat offered by a conservatory, large window or greenhouse – but consider their ultimate heights before planting them.

Purchasing plants
Some shrubs and trees will be available to buy as bare-root plants, which are supplied in the dormant season with no pot of compost around the roots. Bare-root plants are usually cheaper than potted specimens, but they are available only in winter. They may also be sold as 'rootballed', which means they have been recently dug up and the roots wrapped in hessian with a small amount of soil or of compost before sale. Potted plants should be tipped out of their pots to check the roots before buying, and the health assessed as for perennial plants (see Purchasing plants, page 13).

Planting
Shrubs and trees will be growing in the ground for a long time, so it makes sense to prepare the site as well as possible before planting. Dig a large hole, 1½–2 times as wide as the top of the pot or root ball, or the flare of the bare roots (the point at which the roots turn into the stems). When planting a tree that is already at least 1.5m/5ft tall, or a climber that will need supports, put in a stake or framework of supports before the plant itself. Fork over the base of the hole, to ensure the ground is not too compacted, and remove any weeds from the vicinity. When planting in a container, partially fill it with multipurpose compost.

Plant so that the root flare is level with the surface of the soil/compost. Fill underneath if necessary to get the plant to the right height, then backfill around the roots. Using a booted heel (or hand for potted plants), firm in the soil around the roots well to ensure good soil–root contact. Then water the plant in thoroughly.

Maintenance
Keep newly planted trees and shrubs well-watered in their first few months until they are established; thereafter water them as needed. An annual mulch of compost around the base (but not touching the stems) should be all the fertilizer that is needed, although potted specimens may benefit from some liquid fertilizer in the growing season, and being repotted annually.

Check plants before buying – each should be established but not root-bound in its pot.

ANNUALS AND BIENNIALS

Annual plants are those that grow from a seed, flower and make seeds, then die all in a single growing season. Biennials take two growing seasons to complete the process, growing foliage only in the first year and then flowering and dying the following spring or summer. Basil, dill, borage, shiso, summer savory and nasturtium are all examples of annual herbs, and biennial herbs include parsley and caraway. There are also some perennials which, in temperate climates or because it makes best use of the plant, are treated as annuals, such as chilli peppers and chicory.

Annuals are an easy way to start growing herbs, as they do not require any long-term investment of time or space and are generally cheaper to buy. They also fill out a garden very quickly, as they are able to grow a lot of foliage in a short time, and are good filler plants before a larger perennial herb garden is able to establish itself.

Purchasing plants
Annuals and biennials are available to buy as seed and, depending on the plant, as young plants. When buying seed, check they are still within their 'sowing date', which will ensure they are viable. Young plants should be healthy and with no sign of pests or diseases. Always buy short and stocky plants, not over-tall and leggy ones, as they will produce better shaped and healthier mature plants. Never purchase young annual plants that are already flowering, as they will die before offering any real harvests.

It is also possible to find quite large potted herbs, and these can be a cheap way to plant annual herbs. Usually, such a pot of herbs is actually several plants all sown together in the same pot. Water the plant well and then remove its pot. Using a knife or teasing the root ball apart by hand, separate out the young plants into four or five groups. Each of these can be planted and, given this extra space, they will grow into significantly bigger plants than if they were left in the original, crowded pot.

Regular cutting of herbs for use in the kitchen will help to keep shrubs to size.

Although bay can grow to a very large tree, it can be restricted, as well as be trained as a standard.

INTRODUCTION TO GROWING HERBS

INTRODUCTION

Sowing

Seed packets now provide a wealth of sowing information: refer to this for the appropriate times of year to sow the seed, what protection to give them and how deep to sow. In general, sow seed as the soil begins to warm in spring (biennials are generally sown later in the growing season) and put the seed at a depth of twice its size.

Alternatively, seed can be sown in pots or trays on a windowsill or other warm, sunny place and raised into young plants that can be potted on before planting out. The easiest method is to use a tray of individual cells or home-made recycled paper pots that are each filled with compost and sown to create 'plug plants'. The root balls of such young plants can be popped out of the tray and easily planted into larger pots or the open ground with minimal root disturbance.

Microleaves

Some annual plants (and a few perennial ones, too) can be sown to harvest as 'microleaves' – the tiny, first or second leaves that a seed produces, which are full of concentrated flavour and nutrients. Prepare a shallow tray of potting compost and cover the whole surface with a sprinkling of seeds, covering with a thin layer of more compost. Water using a rose attachment or mist thoroughly with a spray bottle. Once the seedlings have reached the desired size, snip off the leaves and discard the compost. Microleaves can be produced year-round from the seeds of basil, nasturtium, fenugreek, chives, dill, coriander, fennel and parsley.

Planting

It is always a good idea to 'harden off' plants raised under cover – whether they are raised from seed or as plug plants. Acclimatizing the plants slowly to the colder conditions will ensure they do not get physiologically shocked, which can set back their growth. To harden off plants, set them outdoors in their pots/trays once the weather has warmed sufficiently that there is minimal risk of frost, but bring them back indoors for the first three or four nights. Then leave the plants out overnight with a covering of newspaper or fleece for another few nights before finally planting them and leaving them without covers. Biennial plants are usually planted out in late summer or early autumn.

When handling young plants, always hold a leaf or the root ball – never the delicate stem, which can be easily crushed, thereby killing the plant. Ensure the soil or compost around the plant is level with the point at which the shoots turn into roots, then firm the soil/compost around the roots well, but

Microleaves are easy to grow and provide an intense herb flavour in a small space.

do not press down around the base of the plant as this can break the roots.

Maintenance
Pinching out the growing tips of annual and biennial plants will make their growth bushier and provide more foliage and flowers for harvest. Do this to young seedlings once they have a few sets of leaves, and continue to do so as they grow. Pinching out flower shoots before the flowers open will prolong the harvest of foliage plants for a few more weeks (the foliage of, for example, basil turns tougher once the plant has flowered). Remove dead plants at the end of the growing season.

HERBS IN THE GROUND
Most herbs will grow best and provide the finest harvests when grown in the ground rather than a pot. There is more space for their roots, and there is less variance in the temperature and moisture levels found there. One exception to this is basil, which prefers the warmth of a windowsill. Although it will grow happily outdoors in a temperate summer, it develops thicker, tougher leaves in the cooler conditions. A windowsill-grown basil provides the tender, paper-thin leaves that grace pizza and salads so well.

HERBS IN THE FLOWER GARDEN
Herb plants are so varied in their shape, flower and form that they can be blended into any style of garden. Fennel and angelica are excellent additions to a herbaceous border, adding graceful height and interesting seed heads. Lavender, bergamot, hyssop, lovage, sweet Cicely and oregano bring colour and foliage to a border. Some herbs such as purple forms of elder and Carolina allspice are regularly listed as 'good plants for the garden' purely for their ornamental value. Herbs can also be planted instead of annual summer bedding – shiso, basil, borage, marigold and dill will provide seasonal colour and foliage as well as a harvest.

HERBS IN THE VEGETABLE PLOT
When planting herbs in the vegetable

Annuals such as comfrey can self-sow around the garden.

Window boxes and pots are ideal for annual and biennial herbs.

INTRODUCTION TO GROWING HERBS

INTRODUCTION

garden, it is best to group annual and perennial herbs and veg together, to avoid disturbing the roots of the perennial plants when the annuals are removed at the end of the season and new ones planted in spring. Herbs can benefit the vegetable garden by attracting pollinators as well as predators of garden pests such as ladybirds and hoverflies, whose larvae love to feast on aphids. Herbs planted among vegetables can also help as companion plants: for example, basil masks the smell of carrots so that the carrot fly cannot find them. Herbs can make productive edging plants for kitchen gardens (see Edging and paths, right). Finally, for the home cook dashing out for ingredients in the rain, it pays to have all the herbs and veg crops in one spot.

A HERB PATCH

An informal herb patch is a charming way to grow a variety of herbs in a small space. Put the tallest plants at the back or (for beds visible from all sides) in the middle of the bed, then layer the

Herbs and vegetables are invaluable planting companions in the garden.

different heights so that the smallest plants are at the front or around the edges of the bed. A herb patch might have a theme – culinary herbs, or cut-flower herbs, for example – or simply be a collection of favourite herb plants.

A FORMAL HERB GARDEN

Herbs are often displayed to their best advantage within a formal herb garden, and the different forms of herbs mean that they can provide both smart lines and more billowing ones within that geometric pattern. Formal herb gardens can take their inspiration from the Elizabethan knot gardens as well as from the continental parterres of the kitchen gardens of the great palaces and houses from the seventeenth to nineteenth centuries, or they can create a more modern look in a narrow bed with lines of the same plant in rows of staggered heights. These gardens often look best with repeating or geometric patterns, a centrepiece (such as a topiary plant or statue) and the use of many of the same herbs to unify the design. Formal herb gardens can look excellent in a small area (perhaps a front garden). However, they use lots of the same herb for the hedges and the repeating patterns, so are not the cheapest in terms of space if they are to provide a varied harvest of herbs.

EDGING AND PATHS

For formal, compact edging to beds, for a kitchen garden or a formal herb garden, introduce herbs that can be clipped and shaped easily, such as lavender, rosemary, thyme and myrtle. More informal hedges and edges can be made from chives, rose, parsley, marigold and salad burnet.

Creeping and low-growing herbs such as creeping thymes and camomile can form a pretty and fragrant informal path when planted at the edges (or sporadically along the path's length in place of paving stones) and allowed to spread to the middle. To keep some hard surface, simply cut back the plants as needed, leaving an undulating path among the plants.

OTHER DESIGN CONSIDERATIONS

When choosing herb plants for a garden, do consider the other users of the space. Children and pets may handle or eat plants that have the potential to be harmful, and spiky plants could potentially cause injury. If the herbs are to be harvested, ensure that they are well away from potential pollutants and contaminants such as roadsides, as well as fields sprayed with chemicals.

INVASIVE HERBS

Although some herbs are invaluable additions to the garden, they spread very quickly or are difficult to eradicate from the soil once planted. They are therefore ideal candidates for container-growing: mint being the best-known example. Give mint plants the largest possible pot, and ensure the compost remains damp. Once the stolons (overground roots) start to spread over the top of the pot, simply snip around the edge to remove them. This method can be used to grow invasive herbs in a garden bed – plant them in a pot, leaving the lip of the pot (preferably plastic so it does not act as a wick) protruding from the soil surface so that the stolons can be easily snipped off.

Invasive herbs of which the root is harvested (for example, horseradish and dandelion) can also be grown in pots, but each pot must be as deep as possible and raised on feet so that the base can be regularly checked for protruding roots that might penetrate paving below.

HERBS IN CONTAINERS

There are many other advantages to growing herbs in pots, even in a large

If space is short, consider growing your herbs in a vertical system of containers.

Sweet violets will happily colonize the ground under trees, where they will suppress weeds.

INTRODUCTION TO GROWING HERBS

INTRODUCTION

garden. Different varieties can be kept separate; invasive plants such as mint can be contained; tender herbs can be easily moved under cover for winter and hardened off again in spring; tropical herbs can be grown indoors; annual ones can be planted without disturbing perennial plants in borders; plants can be placed near seating areas for the best enjoyment of their fragrance; and they can be used for aesthetic effects, such as a pair of topiary bay trees either side of a doorway. Good herbs for outdoor containers include basil, bay, lemon verbena, mint, lavender, rosemary, horseradish, chillies, coriander, saffron, lemongrass, oregano, marjoram, parsley, scented pelargonium, thyme, dandelion and nasturtium.

Choosing containers
In general, it is best to use the biggest possible container for the plant that is to go in it, to provide the maximum root space. However, a young plant will be swamped in a large container,

Pots of herbs grouped together minimizes water loss and wind damage in hot or windy weather.

so put it in a small pot and build up the size of its container year on year by replanting for 3–4 years until it is large enough to go into its final pot.

All containers should have drainage holes and ideally be raised off the ground with pot 'feet', to aid drainage. Terracotta and wooden containers will lose water faster than plastic and metal ones; and metal containers can (if in direct sun) 'fry' the roots of plants in hot summers.

Compost and planting
Most herbs will thrive in multipurpose peat-free compost. If your plants prefer a well-drained environment, mix some grit with the compost. Plant up a container in the same way as planting in the ground (see Planting, page 14). When combining a number of plants in a single pot – for example when underplanting a standard bay tree with a carpet of camomile, or combining a number of annuals within one pot – take into account the plants' heights and spreads. The more plants there are in a pot the more watering and feeding they will require.

GROWING HERBS INDOORS
Good herbs for indoor containers include chillies, lemongrass, scented pelargoniums, turmeric, ginger, black pepper and lemon verbena.

The same principles apply for growing in containers indoors as outside – give the plant plenty of space, water and fertilizer as appropriate. When growing indoors, take into account the light levels (it may be necessary to rotate pots regularly to prevent them leaning towards the light) as well as whether the room is sufficiently warm to grow the plants desired. Check regularly for pests and diseases, and repot annually.

Some herbaceous perennial herbs can be brought indoors to continue growing through winter. Simply divide a portion of mint, or chives, from the main plant in late summer – ensuring there is a good root-to-shoot ratio – and pot on into fresh compost. Place the container on a sunny, warm windowsill. The foliage of these indoor plants will persist even when the plant outside has died back for the year.

Caring for potted herbs
The fertilizers in compost are usually exhausted by the plant within about six months, so plants will need providing with nutrients in another form through the growing season. This could be by mixing controlled-release granules of fertilizer into the surface compost or by applying a liquid feed; either way, follow the instructions on the packet for the correct dosage because too much fertilizer can be toxic for plants.

Each year, take the plants out of their pots, crumble off as much old compost as possible and then replant them in fresh potting compost. This will benefit the plants considerably.

Herbs can be planted informally among other plants such as in this vegetable garden . . .

. . . or en masse as more formal edging, which can also make maintenance easier.

INTRODUCTION TO GROWING HERBS

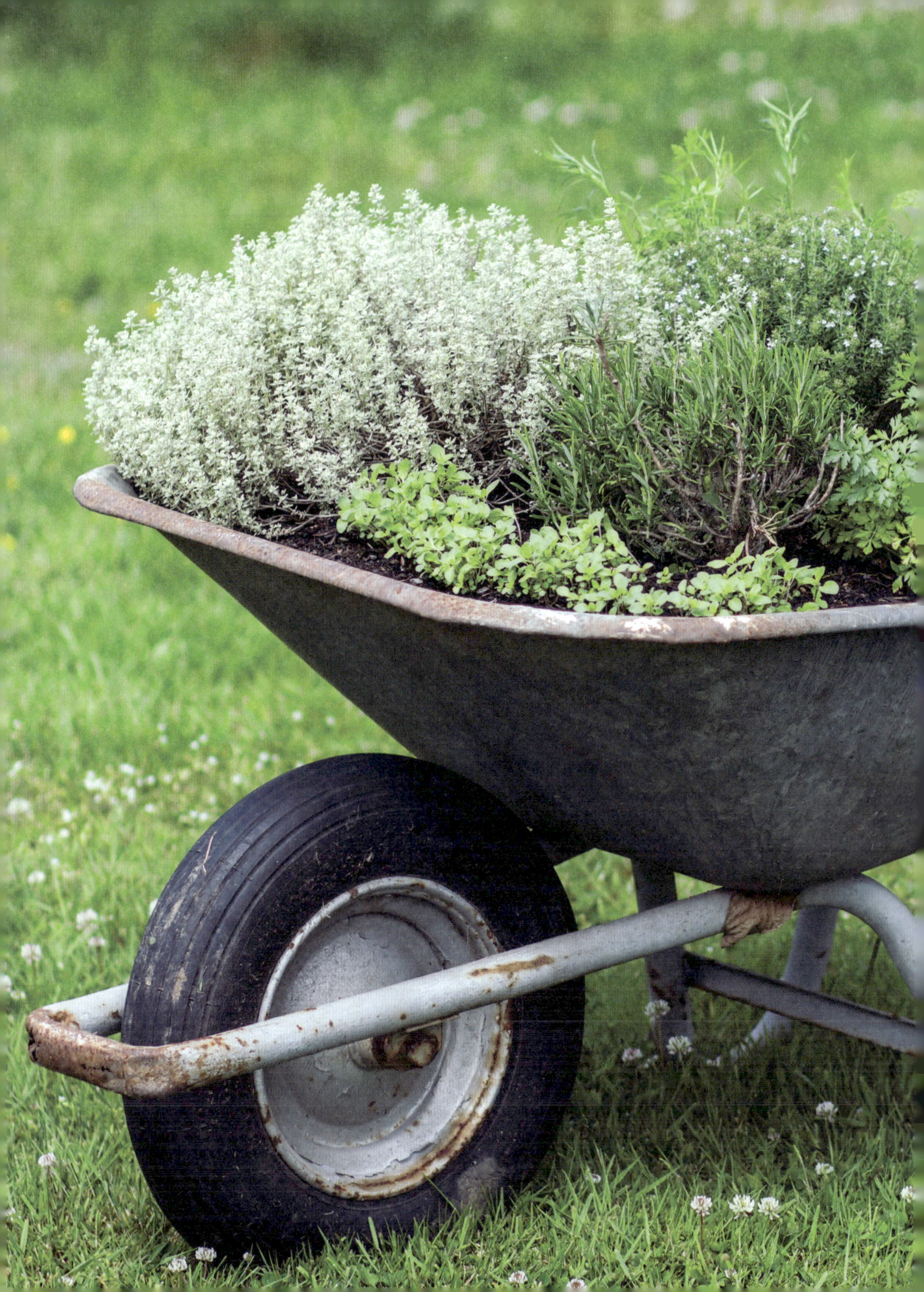

Plants
—

HERBACEOUS PERENNIAL

English mace
Achillea ageratum aka maudlin, sweet milfoil, flossflower, sweet Nancy

Achilles gives his name to this genus, after using it to dress battlefield wounds – yarrow (*A. millefolium*) having many medicinal uses and being an attractive border perennial, too. Meanwhile, English mace is an aromatic addition to other culinary herbs, and its flowers are beloved by pollinating insects.

Family Asteraceae
Height 30–45cm/12–18in
Spread 30cm/12in
Hardiness Zone 7

HOW TO USE
English mace leaves can be used on their own, chopped and sprinkled over potato and rice or be added to pasta dishes. They also go well when combined with other herbs as an infusion in chicken and fish dishes, soups and stews.

HOW TO GROW
Grow in an open, sunny site, and support the tall stems in exposed conditions. English mace tolerates most soils but prefers a well-drained position. Cut back to the ground after flowering, to encourage a second flush of stems, and again in late winter, to remove the dead top growth.

HOW TO HARVEST
Gather leaves, as required; and freeze fresh individual leaves. Flowering and leafy stems can be cut and hung upside down to dry.

CUT OR DRIED
English mace is ideal for cutting in a vase as the delicate foliage accentuates displays. Alternatively, you can cut and dry it, then use it well into winter in teas.

ANNUAL

Electric daisy

Acmella oleracea aka toothache plant, Pará cress

Family Asteraceae
Height 40–70cm/16–28in
Spread 40–70cm/16–28in
Hardiness Zone 2

This annual tends to be grown mostly for its curiosity value and for surprising visitors to the garden. Biting into a flower head produces a shock-like and fizzing sensation in the mouth, which then has a numbing effect, proving why this plant is known both as electric daisy and toothache plant. The sensation is caused by spilanthol, a chemical component of the plant that is also of interest for use as an insecticide.

HOW TO USE
Raw leaves and flower heads can be eaten, but as there is currently limited safety data on consumption of this plant you should taste it only as a curio rather than using it as an ingredient.

HOW TO GROW
Full sun and well-drained soil will suit electric daisy best; this can be in the ground or in a large pot, preferably in a greenhouse. Remove the dead plant in autumn and sow new seed in spring.

HOW TO HARVEST
Pick leaves and flowers to use fresh, as required.

BETTER THAN BOTOX?
Apart from numbing gums, spilanthol in acmella is also being trialled as a safer alternative to Botox. When applied topically, it may relax wrinkles caused by tense facial muscles. In a clinical study, 75 per cent of patients noticed the smoothing effects one day after the first application.

HERBACEOUS PERENNIAL

Anise hyssop
Agastache foeniculum

Tall spikes of pale purple flowers borne over several weeks make this an attractive garden plant, for bees and butterflies as much as for the gardener. Indeed, honey made purely from anise hyssop nectar has a slight aniseed taste.

Family Lamiaceae
Height 45–60cm/18–24in
Spread 30cm/12in
Hardiness Zone 3

HOW TO USE
Leaves can be added raw to salads or to make a sweet and fragrant tea, and the flowers can be put in salads, fruit dishes and drinks.

HOW TO GROW
Thrives in rich soil with plenty of moisture (although anise hyssop is more forgiving of its situation than other *Agastache* species) and full sun. Cover with fleece or a layer of mulch in areas that are likely to experience temperatures below −5°C/23°F, or grow in a large pot that can be moved to an unheated greenhouse for protection. Cut back dead stems in late spring. Plants can be short-lived, and are best propagated by division or cuttings.

HOW TO HARVEST
Use leaves as required, or freeze fresh individual leaves. Flowering and leafy stems can be cut and hung upside down to dry before being stored.

COUGH REMEDY
Anise hyssop leaves are a traditional remedy for bronchial complaints for some Native Americans, and they also have several culinary applications.

HERBACEOUS PERENNIAL

Chives
Allium schoenoprasum

Family Alliaceae
Height 10–60cm/4–24in
Spread 30cm/12in
Hardiness Zone 6

A staple in many herb gardens, chives' grassy form adds a different texture and fresh green look to a bed. Chives grow well in containers, too. Plant *A. schoenoprasum* f. *albiflorum* for a white-flowered variety.

HOW TO USE
The leaves start their fresh growth early in spring and are excellent with potatoes, cheese and eggs. The flowers are also edible, with a milder onion flavour than the leaves.

HOW TO GROW
Chives flourish in partial shade and wetter soil than many other herbs will tolerate, but they also do well in a sunny, dry position. Cut back to the ground after flowering, to stimulate production of fresh leaves (which can become woody if left uncut) and prevent self-sowing. Repeat in autumn once the leaves have died back. Small potted divisions can be overwintered indoors to extend the harvesting season. Divide large clumps in spring.

HOW TO HARVEST
Cut leaves and flowers as needed.

THE ALLIUM FAMILY
Comprising around 700 species, the *Allium* family is one of the oldest known in cultivation. As well as onions, shallots, garlic, leeks and chives, there are many ornamental *Allium* such as *A. cristophii*, with its huge, starry flower heads and decorative seed heads.

OLD AS ONIONS
There are records of onions being used as long ago as 3000 BC, and garlic was found in the tomb of Tutankhamun.

CHIVES

PROJECT 1

A vertical herb garden

Vertical gardens can bring beautiful greenery and fragrance to the smallest of gardens and homes. Ideal for fences or sunny walls – indoors or out – they can be as small as a single, mounted pot or as large as the wall or fence itself. Most proprietary vertical gardens provide the means of securing pots to the wall, or else they comprise fabric pouches. However, with a bit of DIY, you could create guttering or pallet gardens and more.

The best plants for a vertical garden depend to an extent on the type of planter. As a general rule, the less space there is for the roots the more drought-resistant the plants need to be. Small bushy plants such as thyme (see page 124) and camomile (see page 52) are ideal for planting in pouches (see opposite), while pots could support larger trailing or upright plants. Annuals such as marigolds (see page 45), chilli peppers (see page 47), basil (see page 90) and nasturtiums (see page 129) would suit all pots well; perennials such as mint (see page 80), lemon balm (see page 79) and lemongrass (see page 64) would also work well as smaller plants, but would need replacing or dividing as they grew older and larger.

When planting a vertical garden, consider the relative heights of the plants and their habits – are they bushy or trailing? – and plant accordingly. For example, in pouch systems, a lot of bushy plants that will grow together into a full 'green wall' is best. Consider also any finishing touches – an old picture frame around plants can be quite effective, and flat frames painted with blackboard paint can also serve as a means of labelling the plants.

Regular picking for use in the kitchen will help keep to vertical garden plants to size. Check the compost regularly to see if it needs watering. Water plants very carefully to avoid the water and compost spilling on to the wall and floor: always wait for the previous glug to sink in before adding any more water. Alternatively, for larger planted walls, consider installing a drip irrigation system. A little liquid feed once a month through spring and summer will help plants keep healthy.

1. Having secured the planter to a wall or fence, fill the base of each pouch with potting compost.
2. Place the plants – here different thymes and camomile – into the pouches and check that the top of each root ball will not sit too high in its pouch.
3. Backfill each pouch with compost to secure the root ball in place.
4. Water very carefully and gradually, to avoid water and compost spilling over the pouch edges.

A VERTICAL HERB GARDEN

HERBACEOUS PERENNIAL

Garlic chives
Allium tuberosum aka Chinese chives

Garlic chives are easily distinguishable from common chives (*A. schoenoprasum*) by their flatter, more linear leaves. Their white flowers appear later in summer than common chives, too, extending the season of interest in the herb garden.

Family Alliaceae
Height 50cm/20in
Spread 40cm/16in
Hardiness Zone 5

HOW TO USE
Add leaves, flower buds and flowers to salads, cheese dishes, soups and stir-fries, but avoid overcooking. The seeds can be sprouted, or harvested unripe or ripe, when they can be pressed to produce oil.

HOW TO GROW
Garlic chives flourish in partial shade and wetter soil than many other herbs tolerate, but they also do well in a sunny, dry position. Cut back to the ground after the leaves have died back in autumn. Small potted divisions can be overwintered indoors, to extend the harvesting season. Divide large clumps in spring.

HOW TO HARVEST
Cut fresh leaves and flowers as needed, pick seeds when unripe or collect ripe by tying a bag over the ripening seed heads (see Harvesting seed heads and fennel pollen, page 68).

ANYTHING GOES
This late-season chive with its mild, garlicky taste is useful for adding to salads, omelettes, sandwiches and cream cheese.

BIENNIAL

Wild garlic

Allium ursinum aka ramsoms, bear's garlic

Wild garlic is easily cultivated in a shady, damp spot in the garden, thriving where little else will grow, but it can become invasive if its spread is not controlled.

Family Alliaceae
Height 40cm/16in
Spread 30cm/12in
Hardiness Zone 7

HOW TO USE
Whole leaves, wilted or fresh, add a delicious flavour to egg, chicken, rice and pasta dishes. They can also be used to make pesto (see Hey pesto!, page 94).

HOW TO GROW
Plant as bulbs 'in the green', or sow seed, in dappled shade and rich, moist soil. Cut back dead leaves in early summer, and remove seed heads to prevent the plants spreading widely (the bulbs will multiply themselves below ground, too, but this spread is slower and more focused in the planting area).

HOW TO HARVEST
Pick the leaves as needed, ensuring some foliage remains on each plant to enable further growth.

SPRING IN THE AIR
The presence of wild garlic in woodland is easy to detect in spring, when the air is filled with its potent garlicky scent.

SHRUB

Lemon verbena
Aloysia citriodora

Family	Verbenaceae
Height	2.5m/8ft
Spread	2.5m/8ft
Hardiness	Zone 3

This is the ultimate lemon-scented herb. The slightly rough, elongated leaves need only be brushed to release their intoxicating fragrance, and the delicate, white flowers make it an attractive specimen for a container or border.

HOW TO USE
Leaves are best enjoyed as an infusion rather than eaten: generally either as a tea, or in a sugar syrup that can then be included in desserts, baking and cocktails.

HOW TO GROW
Thrives in a hot, sunny site with well-drained soil, where it will overwinter happily (it is deciduous). In colder gardens you may need to grow it in a pot, placed in a sunny spot for summer and moved into a greenhouse or indoors in winter. Prune back to a framework of strong stems about 30cm/12in long in spring; regular picking will encourage fresh shoots and keep this shrub in shape. Plants grown under cover year-round can suffer from greenhouse pests.

HOW TO HARVEST
Pick fresh leaves as required. Dry leaves can also be harvested for tea.

INFUSED SUGAR SYRUPS
Making flavoured syrups is easy, and they can be stored for several weeks to use in drinks, baking and desserts. Simply mix equal quantities of granulated or caster sugar and water (e.g. for 100g/3½oz sugar use 100ml/3½fl oz water) in a saucepan over a low heat until the sugar is dissolved. Bring to a gentle simmer, then remove from the heat and add fresh herbs or flowers, stirring them in. The more herbs used, the stronger the syrup – a handful is a good starting point for around 200g/7oz sugar – but herb quantity will also depend on the intensity of the herb's flavour, so experiment. Cover and leave to infuse for at least an hour, then strain off the syrup and bottle it. Store in the refrigerator.

ANNUAL

Dill
Anethum graveolens

Dill is a herb with a rich history, having been widely used by many ancient and modern cultures for a variety of ailments and problems, from whooping cough to witchcraft.

Family Apiaceae
Height 90cm/36in
Spread 20cm/8in
Hardiness Zone 4

HOW TO USE
Leaves can be chopped and a little added to egg, potato and fish dishes, or be included in mayonnaise as a flavouring. It can be pickled with cucumber, too. The lime-yellow flowers are a pretty addition to cut-flower posies, and seeds can be infused in water for medicinal purposes.

HOW TO GROW
Dill is most easily cultivated from seed. Plant it in a sunny position and a light soil with good drainage for quick flower and seed production, or delay flowering for a short while by placing in dappled shade. Successional sowing ensures a good supply of leaves through spring and summer. Remove dead plants in autumn. Support plants by growing them in groups through peasticks, or else stake individual plants.

HOW TO HARVEST
Cut the fresh leafy fronds and flowers as needed throughout spring and summer. Seed can be harvested in summer (see page 68).

FEATHER STATUES
Watch out for dill in the herbaceous border – its attractive feathery fronds stand tall above many other herbs and perennials. Dill is valued for its airy transparency and beautiful bronze colour.

DILL

HERBACEOUS PERENNIAL

Angelica

Angelica archangelica aka archangel, holy ghost, St Michael's flower

A herb with connections to the heavens, angelica and its related species have long been prized as a medicinal tonic around the world and it was popular in medieval Europe as a plant that could ward off evil.

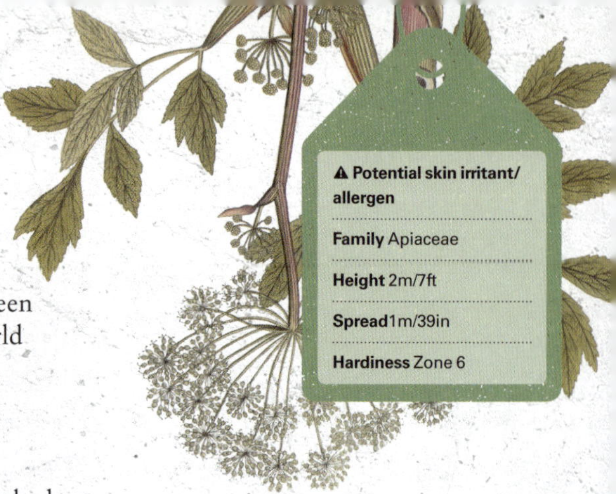

⚠ **Potential skin irritant/allergen**

Family Apiaceae

Height 2m/7ft

Spread 1m/39in

Hardiness Zone 6

HOW TO USE
The young, tender stems can be stewed or baked to add sweetness to fruit dishes, especially rhubarb, or be candied to decorate cakes or to eat as sweets. The huge umbels of lime-green flowers borne on tall stems make it just as useful as an ornamental plant as a herb.

HOW TO GROW
Providing the soil is moist and rich, angelica grows in light conditions ranging from full sun to full shade. It will not flower until its second year, and some specimens may die after flowering or are at least short-lived perennials, so it is best treated as a biennial with young plants kept in reserve.

HOW TO HARVEST
Cut the tender, young stems in late spring and early summer.

CULPEPER'S HERBAL
Nicholas Culpeper (1616–1654) was a physician and apothecary who catalogued an A–Z of all known herbs and their potential medical uses at the time, often not holding back his opinions on modern medicine. His most successful book, *The English Physician*, now known as *Culpeper's Herbal*, is rightly a classic in botanical and herbal literature. When writing on angelica, Culpeper uses the opportunity to compare his fellow physicians to apes – 'though they cannot come off half so cleverly' – and details that angelica will, among many other things, resist 'poison, by defending and comforting the heart, blood, and spirits; it doth the like against the plague and all epidemical diseases'.

BIENNIAL

Chervil
Anthriscus cerefolium

Chervil deserves better recognition as a herb that is not only tasty in its own right, but also one which has the power to enhance the flavours of other herbs when used in combination. It is an ideal choice for a partially shaded herb garden.

Family Apiaceae
Height 60cm/24in
Spread 30cm/12in
Hardiness Zone 4

HOW TO USE
The leaves can be chopped and used fresh in any main dish that benefits from its aniseed-parsley flavour, either raw or added at the very end of cooking. Scatter the chopped leaves over freshly cooked vegetables.

HOW TO GROW
Grow from seed in spring, in rich, moist soil and partial shade. Excess sun or drought can cause chervil to run to seed. Sow successional rows to ensure a regular supply of leaves, although each plant will re-sprout several times after cutting. With protection from a cloche, it will crop well into winter. Remove plants and sow afresh each year.

HOW TO HARVEST
Pick fresh leaves as required.

FINES HERBES
Central to much of French haute cuisine since (before, even) the time of Auguste Escoffier (1846–1935), 'fines herbes' are a combination of fresh parsley, tarragon, chives and chervil leaves. They are used in the classic recipe *omelette aux fines herbes*, which is indeed a delicious way of enjoying these early summer herbs. Over the years the constituent ingredients of fines herbes have been challenged, but for the authentic (and best) taste use the original four herbs.

BIENNIAL

Celery leaf
Apium graveolens var. *dulce*

Distinct from the vegetable celery grown for its crunchy stalks, leaf celery is taxonomically different only by cultivar name. Its stalks are shorter and, as only the leaves are eaten, it can be treated as a cut-and-come-again crop.

Family Apiaceae
Height 30cm/12in
Spread 30cm/12in
Hardiness Zone 4

HOW TO USE
This herb adds a mild celery flavour to salads and is especially good in those accompanying cheese boards. The stems are also edible and best cut when young and tender.

HOW TO GROW
Sow seed annually – the leaves are not as fresh-tasting in the plant's second year – in rich, moist soil in partial shade. Keep the soil moist. Remove any flower stems appearing in the first year (this is likely to be as a result of drought), and discard the plant in favour of fresh sowings in the following spring. Celery leaf can crop into winter if it is given protection from a cloche.

HOW TO HARVEST
Pick leaves and cut stems as required.

DECORATIVE LEAVES
Evidence that the ancient Egyptians used celery leaves to make garlands has been found in tombs around 3,000 years old.

GROWING HERBS

HERBACEOUS PERENNIAL

Horseradish

Armoracia rusticana aka pepper root

Family	Brassicaceae
Height	1m/39in
Spread	1m/39in
Hardiness	Zone 6

Once established, horseradish is very difficult to eradicate completely from a garden, so it may be advisable to plant it in a deep pot to prevent its spread. Raise the pot on 'feet' or other supports so that any roots emerging from the base can be cut off, as they are liable to penetrate any ground or even paving beneath.

HOW TO USE
Although the young leaves can be eaten raw or – for a milder taste – wilted, it is for the pungent root that horseradish is generally grown. It can be preserved as horseradish sauce and chrain, and is particularly good with meat, fish and beetroot dishes.

HOW TO GROW
Moist soil in partial shade is horseradish's preferred habitat. Any leaves that die off in autumn can be pulled off and composted.

HOW TO HARVEST
Pick young leaves in spring and summer. Roots can be harvested at any time of year, but have their best flavour in autumn. Dig out the top 20–30cm/8–12in of root (or as much as can be extricated from the soil) and use promptly.

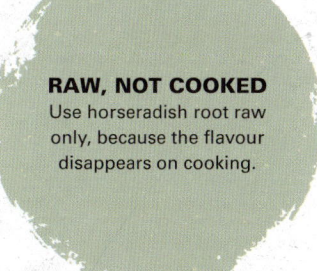

RAW, NOT COOKED
Use horseradish root raw only, because the flavour disappears on cooking.

HORSERADISH 37

SUBSHRUB OR PERENNIAL

French tarragon

Artemisia dracunculus aka tarragon, biting dragon

Coming from the wormwood family, from which the alcohols absinthe and vermouth are made, some *Artemisia* species contain powerful compounds used variously to repel insects and to combat malaria and poisonous bites (hence this tarragon's alternative common name 'biting dragon'). French tarragon is the better culinary choice than the hardier, but more strident, Russian tarragon (*A. dracunculus* subsp. *dracunculoides*).

Family Asteraceae
Height 1.5m/5ft
Spread 60cm/24in
Hardiness Zone 6

HOW TO USE
Fresh chopped leaves can flavour mayonnaise or creamy sauces; it is perfect with chicken, too. Tarragon leaves can be made into a cordial known as tarhun.

HOW TO GROW
Plant in well-drained soil in full sun or partial shade. Tarragon can be susceptible to cold winter wet, so is better planted in a pot that can be overwintered under cover. Cut back to the ground in late winter. Replace plants after two years for the freshest-tasting leaves.

HOW TO HARVEST
Pick leaves (or whole stems of leaves for stuffing chicken) as required.

> **'HENRY VIII DIVORCED CATHERINE OF ARAGON FOR HER RECKLESS USE OF TARRAGON'**
> Whomever wrote this couplet attributed to Ogden Nash, it would seem that matters of state and the heart could not provide as satisfactory a rhyme with 'Aragon' as the name of the popular Tudor herb.

GROWING HERBS

HERBACEOUS PERENNIAL

Orach

Atriplex hortensis aka mountain spinach

Orach can fast turn into a weed of cultivated soil if allowed to go to seed, but providing this is averted it is a far easier crop than spinach and other leafy greens.

Family Amaranthaceae
Height 1m/39in
Spread 50cm/20in
Hardiness Zone 2

HOW TO USE
Young leaves can be eaten raw in salads, while older leaves can be wilted and cooked in any recipe that calls for spinach.

HOW TO GROW
The best plants and leaves are produced on rich soil in full sun or dappled shade (especially for the red variety, which can scorch easily). Pinch out the growing tips (and eat), to encourage bushy plants; and pull up plants once they start flowering. Sow fresh seed for new plants the following spring.

HOW TO HARVEST
Pick leaves as required.

PRETTY CROP
For an especially attractive crop, grow *Atriplex hortensis* 'Rubra', which has attractive purple-red leaves.

39

PROJECT 2

Herb oils, vinegars, spirits and waters

A little herb goes a long way in the kitchen, and many different herbs can be preserved and introduced into oils, vinegars, spirits and waters. All these infusions are incredibly easy to make, and are delicious or fragrant.

HERB OILS
Fill a clean, sterilized bottle with good-quality olive oil, allowing some space at the top for the volume of herbs. Pack in the herbs (rosemary, thyme, sage, oregano or a mix of some or all of these); consider the look as well as the flavour when giving as a gift. The sealed bottles should be stored in a cool, dry place and consumed within six months.

CHILLI OIL
Select narrow or small chillies that will fit into the bottle when halved. The hotter the chilli, the stronger the oil. Halve the chillies lengthways and push into the bottle. Heat good-quality olive oil to around 40°C/104°F and pour over the chillies. Seal and leave to infuse for two weeks, then strain and re-bottle only the oil. A whole chilli can be added to the bottle as decoration. Store in a cool, dry place and use within six months, taking out the chilli once the bottle is opened (it may be necessary to decant it).

HERB VINEGARS
Fill a clean, sterilized bottle with good-quality cider or white wine vinegar, allowing some space at the top for the volume of herbs. Pack in the herbs (tarragon, fennel, thyme, chives, parsley, cloves, ginger or a mix of some or all of these; try herb flowers, too, such as thyme), shake gently and seal. Store in a cool, dark place for a month, then strain out the herbs and re-bottle only the vinegar. Store in a cool, dry place and consume within a year.

INFUSED ALCOHOLS
Herbs as well as the more traditional fruits such as raspberries and sloes can add flavours to spirits. Simply add sprigs of fresh herbs to a bottle of vodka, gin or rum and leave to infuse. Good herbs to source include thyme, rosemary, lemon verbena, mint, lavender, basil, lemongrass and dill. A few threads of saffron imbue a golden yellow colour, as well. To make chilli vodka, slice the chillies in half lengthways before infusing, and strain after two weeks. Whole chillies can be added to the strained vodka for decoration. See also Herbs for cocktails, page 104.

SCENTED WATERS
Steep a small handful of fresh or dried herbs – lavender, mint, lemony herbs and scented pelargoniums are especially effective – in 500ml/17½fl oz of just-off-boiled water for five minutes, then strain into a bottle. Use as a fabric spray when ironing, within one month.

MAKING HERB OIL
1. Pour good-quality olive oil into a clean, sterilized bottle or bottles.
2. Select one or more types of herb and ensure each is fresh and disease-free.
3. Push the herbs into each bottle; the more herbs used, the stronger the flavour will be in the oil.
4. Seal, then leave to infuse for two weeks before using. Remove the herbs once the bottle is opened.

HERB OILS, VINEGARS, SPIRITS AND WATERS

HERBACEOUS PERENNIAL

Good King Henry

Blitum bonus-henricus aka all good, Lincolnshire asparagus

Good King Henry is distantly related to the common garden weed fat hen (*Chenopodium album*). A naturally leafy crop, it can alternatively be grown as a 'poor man's asparagus'.

Family Amaranthaceae
Height 60cm/24in
Spread 45cm/18in
Hardiness Zone 7

HOW TO USE
The leaves, which are rich in iron and other nutrients, can be enjoyed raw or cooked like spinach. Shoots and flower spikes can be blanched or otherwise cooked quickly like asparagus.

HOW TO GROW
Good King Henry produces its best leafy growth in rich, well-drained soil in full sun, but will grow in most positions. Easily divided, a patch is best refreshed with new plants every three years. To grow it like asparagus, in spring cover the emerging shoots with soil or a rhubarb forcer. Cut back dead top growth in autumn.

HOW TO HARVEST
Pick leaves and cut flower spikes as required. Cut shoots of plants grown like asparagus when they are around 15cm/6in long.

ROYAL PATRON
Although the origins of the common name Good King Henry are lost in the mists of time, the most widely agreed version is that the 'king' part of the epithet was applied later, perhaps as a way of making it more appealing an ingredient: spinach with royal approval, so to speak. Good Henry (Guter Heinrich) seems to have been a fairy or helpful goblin in medieval central Europe, associated with hedgerows where the plant would grow, and perhaps the plant was named after him. It also helps to distinguish Good King Henry from Bad Henry (Böser Heinrich), a poisonous plant.

GROWING HERBS

ANNUAL

Borage

Borago officinalis aka starflower, cool tankard

More often used to adorn cocktails such as Pimms than tankards, borage is nonetheless a 'cool' ingredient to decorate both drinks and food. The white-flowered version, *B. officinalis* 'Alba', is also very attractive and slightly shorter, being 60cm/24in tall.

⚠ **Potential skin irritant/allergen**

Family Boraginaceae
Height 1m/39in
Spread 30cm/12in
Hardiness Zone 5

HOW TO USE
Borage's electric-blue flowers are edible, and have a mild cucumber taste. Use them to decorate drinks, as well as sweet and savoury dishes such as salads and gazpacho. They can also be frozen into ice cubes (see Herbs for cocktails, page 104) and crystallized. Young leaves have a cucumber taste, too – their prickles dissolve in the mouth.

HOW TO GROW
This herb prefers well-drained soil and full sun, but the richer the soil the larger the plant. Support plants as they can easily flop over once at their full height. Deadhead or pick regularly to ensure longer flowering. Remove dead plants in autumn: once sown or planted in a garden, borage will happily self-sow the following season's plants.

HOW TO HARVEST
Pick flowers and young leaves as needed.

HANDLE WITH CARE
Wear gloves when handling borage because its leaves and stems are covered in small prickles.

BORAGE

HERBACEOUS PERENNIAL

Mustard
Brassica juncea

Family	Brassicaceae
Height	1m/39in
Spread	30cm/12in
Hardiness	Zone 5

The pungency of mustard has long been considered useful to alleviate minor ailments, particularly those associated with chilly weather. Its warming properties in a footbath, for example, are a traditional remedy for colds.

HOW TO USE
Although mustard leaves can be eaten raw, wilted or cooked, and also pickled, it is generally for the seeds (and the oil that can be extracted from them) that the plant is grown commercially. Young seed pods can be eaten raw or preserved, and seeds can be enjoyed dry or sprouted.

HOW TO GROW
Grow in full sun and rich, well-drained soil (a slightly alkaline pH of 7–8 helps, as with all brassicas, to prevent clubroot disease). Sow annually in spring, and remove dead plants during autumn.

HOW TO HARVEST
Pick young leaves and tender seed pods as required. Harvest seed when ripe (see also page 68).

GREEN MUSTARD
Gardeners sometimes grow mustard as a green manure. It acts as a mulch and covers the soil to suppress weeds between crops. The mustard plants are cut down when fully grown, and left to wither on the surface before being dug into the soil.

ANNUAL

Marigold
Calendula officinalis aka pot marigold

There are few brighter or sunnier flowers than the marigold, which brings colour, pollinators and edible flowers to a vegetable garden from spring to early autumn.

Family Asteraceae
Height 40–50cm/16–20in
Spread 40–50cm/16–20in
Hardiness Zone 5

HOW TO USE
The flower petals can be scattered raw over salads and rice dishes or used to decorate cakes. When cooked, marigold petals add colour to rice (it is sometimes adopted as a saffron substitute), dairy products and soups.

HOW TO GROW
Sow in well-drained soil in full sun. Deadhead regularly, as once planted it will happily self-sow around the garden. Remove dead plants in autumn.

HOW TO HARVEST
The flowers are sensitive to the weather, and will close up in damp or cold conditions so aim to harvest on a warm, sunny day. Pick flowers as required and remove the petals for consumption only.

MEDICINAL USES
Marigold is also widely added to herbal medicine, particularly to creams and balms for soothing skin.

SHRUB

Carolina allspice

Calycanthus floridus aka spicebush, sweet shrub

This attractive, large, deciduous shrub bears glossy leaves and fragrant, crimson-red flowers that resemble magnolia flowers.

HOW TO USE
Being a more manageable and hardier plant than cinnamon, the powdered bark of Carolina allspice is an acceptable substitute for cinnamon, and boasts hints of clove as well.

HOW TO GROW
When planted in full sun, it grows happily in most soils. Carolina allspice can be cut back after flowering, to restrict its size if required, in addition to the main prune after harvesting.

HOW TO HARVEST
Cut the driest-looking branches from mid- to late summer. Peel off the bark and leave it to dry in a warm, sunny, dry spot (such as a windowsill). Once fully dry the bark can be stored in an airtight container and be ground to a powder as needed, using a spice grinder or pestle and mortar.

⚠ Flowers and fruit are poisonous
Family Calycanthaceae
Height 3m/10ft
Spread 3m/10ft
Hardiness Zone 5

CULINARY ALTERNATIVE
Carolina allspice can be introduced in any dish that would otherwise include cinnamon – from apple pie to porridge.

ANNUAL OR PERENNIAL

Chilli pepper

Capsicum annuum aka chillies

Natives of South America, from where they spread to Asia, Africa and beyond in the Middle Ages, chillies are ubiquitous in any spicy dish. Whether they are used to add a subtle flavour or a raging heat there is a chilli to suit every taste and palate, although the widest variety is generally available only by growing one's own plants from seed.

Family Solanaceae
Height 0.3–1.5m/1–5ft
Spread 50–100cm/ 20–39In
Hardiness Zone 1c–2

HOW TO USE
Whether raw or cooked, the fruits of the chilli pepper can be added to savoury and sweet dishes and also to drinks. It is the white pith that contains the highest capsaicin levels, not the seeds, so remove both if desired.

HOW TO GROW
Although a chilli plant is actually a perennial, in temperate climates it is more easily treated as an annual, sown in late winter and discarded after harvesting the last fruits in autumn. Plants grown with protection throughout their lives generally fare better than those left exposed. Chilli seeds need a heated propagator or a similar set-up to germinate. Seedlings should be potted on until planting in their final positions in full sun and rich, well-drained soil (in a large pot or the open ground). Do this in late spring for plants grown under cover (greenhouse, windowsill, cloche or polytunnel) and in early summer once there is minimal risk of frost for plants outdoors.

ANNUAL OR PERENNIAL

Stake plants to provide their often-heavy branches with support. Aphids and whitefly may affect plants, so remove or deal with the problem as soon as it is seen.

HOW TO HARVEST
When a chilli pepper is firm to a gentle squeeze around the base of its stalk, it is mature and can be harvested. For the full flavour profile and any extra heat to develop, leave a chilli to ripen to its final colour. The fruit and its stalk should snap easily from the branch. Eat fresh, or preserve for later use. Chillies can be dried, frozen or infused into oils and spirits (see also Herb oils, vinegars, spirits and waters, page 40).

FEEL THE BURN
The heat of a chilli is produced by chemicals called capsaicinoids, especially the alkaloid capsaicin. The original measurement of a chilli's heat was the Scoville test, devised in 1912 by Wilbur Scoville. This measures the capsaicin level in a chilli in Scoville Heat Units (SHU), but relies on (brave) tasters to determine the dilution at which the burn is no longer apparent. Although the Scoville test is less accurate than modern methods of chemical analysis to measure capsaicin content, it is still the most widely adopted among self-professed chilli fanatics.

Breeding by professionals and amateurs continues in greenhouses around the world, to create the next hottest chilli. Usually the focus is on the habanero (Scotch bonnet) types, specifically the 'Naga' strain. An average jalapeño chilli measures at most 5,000 SHU; in recent years the 'Dorset Naga' broke the 1 million SHU barrier, and since then even the 'Dorset Naga' has been surpassed.

ANNUAL OR PERENNIAL

NOTABLE CULTIVARS

'Aji Limon'
Yellow fruits have a distinct lemon flavour. Its cascading form is suitable for hanging baskets and container growing.

'Anaheim'
A medium-hot chilli, very good for stuffing, used (when dried and ground) to make paprika.

'Apricot'
A relatively mild habanero. The best chilli for tasting the real fruitiness of the pepper rather than purely heat.

'Cayenne'
Long, thin peppers of high heat levels, used commercially for dried chilli flakes and ground chilli powder.

'Cherry Bomb'
A dumpy, red chilli good for stuffing and salsa; it has a medium heat level.

'Hungarian Hot Wax'
A mild and crunchy chilli suitable for stir-frying; the name emphasizes the importance of the chilli-growing industry in Hungary.

CHILLI PEPPER   49

ANNUAL OR PERENNIAL

'Jalapeño'
The main chilli sold (often purely as 'red' or 'green' chillies) in supermarkets, the medium-hot jalapeño is popular in Mexican cuisine.

'NuMex Twilight'
A compact plant with a profusion of tiny, relatively hot fruits ripening from purple through orange and yellow to red, so that the plant displays all the colours at the same time.

'Pimientos de Padron'
A very mild chilli traditionally picked green and flash-fried in oil and salt, to eat warm as a bar snack.

'Poblano'
A very mild and very large, flattish pepper, traditionally picked green then stuffed and baked; it is also known as an ancho chilli when picked red and is excellent when smoked.

BIENNIAL

Caraway
Carum carvi

Family	Apiaceae
Height	90cm/36in
Spread	30cm/12in
Hardiness	Zone 5

Caraway may aid digestion, which might explain its traditional inclusion in heavy and rich dishes such as goulash, sausages and cheese. Its spice-like flavour is added to drinks such as kümmel, too, as well as to foods such as sauerkraut. Despite its widespread use in northern and eastern Europe today, caraway originates from Asia, and caraway seeds have been found in Stone Age sites.

HOW TO USE
The leaves can be eaten raw in salads or cooked in soups, while the long taproots are cooked as vegetables. Seeds are added to dishes such as those described above and to cakes and biscuits.

HOW TO GROW
Sow direct in a sunny position. Caraway tolerates most soils. Remove dead plants after seed has ripened in the second year.

HOW TO HARVEST
Pick leaves as required in the first year. Harvest ripe seed (see also page 68) for drying, and cut off the root for cooking having dug up the plant.

HERB LORE
In the Middle Ages caraway had many cooking uses and was even the ingredient of love potions, as it was thought to promote constancy.

CARAWAY 51

PERENNIAL

Camomile

Chamaemelum nobile aka Roman camomile

The botanical name of this herb derives from the Greek *chamaimēlon*, meaning 'earth apple', a slightly odd name to look at the plant but explained by the apple-like scent of the evergreen foliage when crushed or stepped on.

⚠ Potential skin irritant/allergen

Family Asteraceae
Height 10cm/4in
Spread 45cm/18in
Hardiness Zone 7

HOW TO USE
The flowers are infused to make camomile tea ('one tablespoonful to be taken at bedtime', according to Beatrix Potter in *The Tale of Peter Rabbit*), which has calming properties. As a fragrant, no-mow lawn, its non-flowering cultivar 'Treneague' is the best choice (see also Herb lawns and seats, page 120).

HOW TO GROW
Prefers light, well-drained soil in full sun. Weed the gaps of camomile lawns until plants are well-established and covering all the ground. Flowering camomile should be cut back after flowering, to keep plants from becoming leggy.

HOW TO HARVEST
Harvest flowers once they are fully open and use fresh, or dry and store (for one year only).

LONG-LIVED FLOWERS
Camomile flowers will prolong the life of other varieties of cut flowers when their flower heads are added to the water.

GROWING HERBS

ANNUAL OR PERENNIAL

Chicory

Cichorium intybus aka succory, witloof, blue sailors

Family	Asteraceae
Height	1.5m/5ft
Spread	75cm/30in
Hardiness	Zone 5

Treading the line between herb, vegetable and ornamental plant, chicory's pretty flowers belie the bitterness of the rest of the plant. Although a perennial, it is usually treated as an annual.

HOW TO USE
Loose-leaved types can be enjoyed raw in salads, or else the 'hearts' of hearting varieties can be eaten raw or lightly charred. Other varieties can be forced for use over winter. The flowers are also edible, as are the roots.

HOW TO GROW
Sow in a sunny or partially shady spot, in light soil (the lighter the soil the easier the harvest of the roots will be). To force chicory, or 'chicons', sow in late summer then cut back all growth in late autumn. Cover with a pot or similar that will exclude all light; harvest after 4–6 weeks.

HOW TO HARVEST
Pick the leaves and flowers, or cut hearts, as required. Loose-leaved varieties can be treated as cut-and-come-again; most hearting types will re-sprout. Harvest forced chicory immediately before use or it will quickly turn limp. Dig up roots in autumn.

CAFÉ CHICORY
The roots of chicory can be dried, roasted and ground for use as a coffee substitute, while the sap can be made into a chewing gum.

PROJECT 3

Herbs as cut flowers

The herb garden is a rich source of home-grown cut flowers, all of which have a guaranteed fragrance as well as pretty blooms. Some herbs bear relatively showy flowers, such as angelica, bergamot and agastache; others have more delicate flowers, such as borage and sweet violets. Still more herbs can be used just with foliage or with their own small flowers as background 'filler' stems, such as dill, marjoram and mint. As well as the overall look, it can be interesting to take the folklore and language of the flowers into account when making up posies: for example, rosemary can be included for remembrance.

HERBS THAT MAKE GOOD CUT FLOWERS

Angelica (*Angelica archangelica*)
Anise hyssop (*Agastache foeniculum*)
Bergamot (*Monarda didyma*)
Borage (*Borago officinalis*)
Dill (*Anethum graveolens*)
English lavender (*Lavandula angustifolia*)
English mace (*Achillea ageratum*)
Feverfew (*Tanacetum parthenium*)
Hyssop (*Hyssopus officinalis*)
Marigold (*Calendula officinalis*)
Marjoram (*Origanum majorana*)
Mint (*Mentha* species), especially apple mint (*M. suaveolens*)
Oregano (*Origanum vulgare*)
Poppy (*Papaver rhoeas*)
Rosemary (*Salvia rosmarinus* syn. *Rosmarinus officinalis*)
Sage (*Salvia officinalis*)
Scented-leaf pelargoniums (*Pelargonium*)
Sweet violet (*Viola odorata*)
Thyme (*Thymus* species)

THE HERB OF LOVE
Myrtle is associated with the ancient goddesses Venus and Aphrodite. A sprig of myrtle is traditionally included in a wedding bouquet. A green-fingered bride could strike that sprig as a cutting, grow it on, and then give sprigs of the new plants to any daughters for their own bouquets and gardens.

HERBS AS CUT FLOWERS 55

TREE

Citrus bergamot

Citrus × *limon* Bergamot Group

Family Rutaceae
Height 10m/33ft
Spread 7m/23ft
Hardiness Zone 1c

Not to be confused with another plant with the same common name of bergamot (*Monarda didyma*; see page 86), the citrus bergamot can be grown in a pot to restrict its size and make it more suitable for a domestic garden or greenhouse.

HOW TO USE
The flowers are a component of neroli oil, which is widely used in perfumery and aromatherapy and is a reputed aphrodisiac. When infused in water, the flowers also provide what is widely known as 'orange blossom water', an ingredient of desserts, cakes and pastries. The fruits can be used as a substitute for limes, and its peel produces bergamot oil.

HOW TO GROW
Cultivate citrus bergamot in well-drained soil in full sun, or in a large pot under cover of a greenhouse, conservatory or similar. Water well in spring and summer, and provide fertilizer for potted trees according to the manufacturer's instructions. Prune in spring, to maintain the shape only.

HOW TO HARVEST
Pick flowers when they first open, for infusing into orange blossom water; pick fruits when ripe for the best oil and fruit fragrance and flavour. Note: oil distillation is unlikely to be effective or economically worthwhile on a domestic scale.

SCENTED OIL
Citrus bergamot fruit peel produces oil, which is also used in aromatherapy and for flavouring Earl Grey tea.

PERENNIAL

Lesser calamint
Clinopodium nepeta

Lesser calamint's flowers are individually insignificant, yet they cover the plant in profusion in summer.

Family Lamiaceae
Height 30–50cm/12–20in
Spread 30cm/12in
Hardiness Zone 5

HOW TO USE
The leaves are powerful, with a flavour somewhere between mint and oregano, and are suitable only with robust flavours such as roast red meats or where some extra flavour is required. They can also be infused to make a tea. Pregnant women should avoid consumption of calamint, because it contains a compound that can cause abortion.

HOW TO GROW
Lesser calamint prefers full sun and well-drained – even dry – soil. Cut back after flowering to stimulate fresh growth in late summer and keep it tidy. The whole plant can be cut back again in autumn or late winter, to keep it compact and bushy. The semi-evergreen stems retain some leaves in mild winters.

HOW TO HARVEST
Pick leaves as required.

ON THE EDGE
Lesser calamint's compact bushiness makes it an ideal candidate to use for edging a herb garden.

ANNUAL

Coriander

Coriandrum sativum aka cilantro, Chinese parsley

Easily mistaken for parsley, until the leaves are crushed to release their distinctive, soapy scent, coriander is an ancient herb with a range of reputed beneficial effects on the digestive system.

Family Apiaceae
Height 60cm/24in
Spread 20cm/8in
Hardiness Zone 5

HOW TO USE
The fresh leaves are a key ingredient in the preparation of much of south-east Asian cuisine, and they also accompany many traditional Mexican dishes very well. The seeds are used whole or ground, to add a gentle spice to Indian curries and in a range of other savoury and sweet foods. The roots, when peeled and blended to a paste or chopped and fried, have a taste more similar to the seed than the leaf.

HOW TO GROW
There are varieties for leaves ('Cilantro') and specifically for seeds ('Morocco'), but the basic form will produce a good crop of both. Sow seed in well-drained soil in full sun, unless you want to enjoy the leaves and roots, in which case you should sow in dappled shade as too much heat and sun can cause plants to bolt (run to seed). Always keep plants well watered. Remove dead plants in autumn.

HOW TO HARVEST
Pick leaves as required. Harvest seed when ripe (see also page 68). Pull up plants to harvest roots in late summer.

TUDOR DELICACY
In sixteenth-century England whole coriander seeds were made into tiny sweets by coating them in many layers of sugar.

CORM

Saffron
Crocus sativus aka saffron crocus

Saffron's labour-intensive harvest – each thread must be picked from the centre of the flower by hand – and the fact that each corm produces only a single flower with a few threads makes it one of the most expensive ingredients on earth.

Family Iridaceae
Height 10cm/4in
Spread 10cm/4in
Hardiness Zone 6

HOW TO USE
Saffron adds a delicate spice and an unmistakable, yellow hue to rice in such dishes as paella and in baked goods. It has a mild mood-enhancing effect that is easily attained by infusion in alcohol.

HOW TO GROW
Plant the corms in late summer in well-drained, light, but rich soil in full sun. Corms flower once they reach 3cm/1¼in across and after six weeks of a warm, dry summer (soil temperatures in excess of 20°C/68°F).

HOW TO HARVEST
Pick the three red, thread-like styles from the centre of each flower with care (use tweezers if necessary). Harvested saffron must be dried before use and storage; consume stored threads within a year – after that the flavour deteriorates.

A RICH HISTORY
Saffron crocus is actually a sterile plant – meaning it will not produce seeds – so it has to be propagated from offsets produced by the parent corm. This means all the saffron crocuses in cultivation, for they are not found in the wild, are clones of each other and of plants grown for at least 4,000 years. Historically saffron crocuses were grown in a few major centres, including Saffron Walden in the UK and Nuremburg in Germany. Most of the world's supplies are now grown in Iran, Greece and Morocco.

PROJECT 4

Herbal tisanes

Having fresh or dried herbs to hand for herbal tea blends year-round is one of the great advantages of a small herb garden. For tea-lovers, an entire herb garden could be designed around simply the best herbs for making tea.

Technically, herbal tea is a 'tisane', as 'tea' refers to the leaves of *Camellia sinensis* (also easily grown in a domestic garden and in cool-temperate climates). Brewing a refreshing and restorative cup of tisane could not be easier: boil some water and leave it to cool for a couple of minutes before pouring it over a few sprigs of fresh herbs in a mug. Leave to infuse for around five minutes, then remove the herbs before drinking the tisane; if preferred, keep the herbs in the mug for a more intense taste.

Although the herbs listed below are the best and most easily grown for tisanes, you should refer to the individual herb entries as well; many more can be enjoyed either fresh or dried. You could also experiment with different blends. Some herbs are reputed to help certain complaints, but you should never consume any herb to excess, and always check for any contra-indications, especially during pregnancy.

HERBS FOR TISANES

- Lemon verbena (*Aloysia citriodora*) has the strongest lemon flavour of all the herbs and makes an excellent tea.
- Camomile (*Chamaemelum nobile*) is a good herb for a bedtime tisane. Being soothing and calming, it may help to induce a sleepy feeling.
- Lemongrass (*Cymbopogon citratus*) has a lemon flavour not unlike lemon sherbet. Chop the long leaves and add to the water in an infuser, or scoop out the leaves before drinking.
- Fennel (*Foeniculum vulgare*), especially the seeds, provides a cleansing tea with a good aniseed taste that is reputed to calm the digestion.
- Lemon balm (*Melissa officinalis*) has a more grassy lemon taste, but when mixed with mint makes a good tea. It is reputed to be good for relieving sad moods.
- Mint (*Mentha* species) is widely known as a tisane, and is considered especially good for the digestion and upset stomachs.
- Nettle (*Urtica dioica*) provides a rather bland but cleansing tisane, and is best mixed with other herbs such as mint or fennel for more flavour.
- Ginger (*Zingiber officinale*) has been used as a traditional remedy for nausea. A slice or two of fresh root is all that is needed.

Beyond the world of basic tisanes, rosehip syrup is excellent when diluted in hot water for a warming drink full of vitamin C, and warm turmeric drinks (often based on milk or milk substitutes, and mixed with other spices such as cinnamon) are gaining in popularity.

HERBAL TISANES

ANNUAL

Cumin
Cuminum cyminum

Family Apiaceae
Height 30cm/12in
Spread 30cm/12in
Hardiness Zone 1c

Enjoyed mainly in Indian and Asian cuisine, the cumin family contains only two species. As with many of the seed-producing herbs (for example, coriander, caraway, fennel) cumin is in the Apiaceae family, which bear umbel flowers beloved by bees.

HOW TO USE
Seeds are added whole or ground to flavour curries and as a spice rub for meat. Oil can also be distilled from the seeds.

HOW TO GROW
Grow in well-drained soil in full sun. If temperatures are not sufficiently high (at least 28°C/82°F for 3–4 months), seed may not ripen. Remove dead plants in autumn.

HOW TO HARVEST
Collect seed when ripe (see also 68).

WEIGHT OF HISTORY
Cumin is mentioned in the Bible (Matthew 23:23) as a means of paying tithes, along with mint and anise.

HERBACEOUS PERENNIAL

Turmeric

Curcuma longa aka haridra

Turmeric used to be viewed as an inexpensive saffron substitute, although it works only as a colourant in that respect because its strong flavour can easily overwhelm a dish. The sunshine-yellow colour of the spice is traditionally used to dye the robes of Buddhist monks.

Family Zingiberaceae
Height 1m/39in
Spread 1m/39in+
Hardiness Zone 1b

HOW TO USE
The powdered rhizome is added to curries and rice dishes as a flavouring and a colourant, and in the milk (or milk-substitute) drink known as a turmeric latte or *haldi doodh*. The leaves can be used to wrap foods for steaming, thereby imparting a delicate fragrance to their contents.

HOW TO GROW
Plant fresh rhizomes (sold as tubers) in well-drained soil or pots. Grow in a warm, humid place in full sun or in dappled shade.

HOW TO HARVEST
Gather the fresh leaves as required. Dig up and cut off sections of rhizome when the plant is dormant; steam or boil them, then dry before grinding into a powder.

HEALTH BENEFITS
Recently the health benefits of turmeric are being rediscovered. The claims are myriad, but further research is needed to confirm any positive effects.

PERENNIAL

Lemongrass
Cymbopogon citratus

An attractive, large plant for a sunny windowsill or greenhouse, lemongrass exudes a scent level similar to that of lemon balm (*Melissa officinalis*) but not as strong as lemon verbena (*Aloysia citriodora*). However, its essential oils are powerful enough to be widely used in lemongrass and other scented perfumes.

Family Poaceae
Height 1.5m/5ft
Spread 1m/39in
Hardiness Zone 1c

HOW TO USE
The fresh leaves provide a lemony flavour to teas, and impart a delicate flavour when wrapped around other foods for steaming. The fleshy base of the leaves can be selected as an aromatic to infuse in coconut-based curries, rice and fish dishes. When dried and ground, lemongrass is known as sereh powder.

HOW TO GROW
Cultivate in well-drained soil or potting compost in full sun. A moderately humid spot is ideal, or else mist regularly. Plants are most quickly grown from divided clumps, but leaf bases bought from food shops can be rooted in a glass of water before potting up.

HOW TO HARVEST
Cut fresh leaves as required. Sever the leaf bases by slicing them cleanly at ground level.

CATNIP
Cats love the pendulous leaves of lemongrass as fragrant playthings, and will quickly shred them into brown tatters.

ANNUAL OR PERENNIAL

Epazote

Dysphania ambrosioides aka Mexican tea, wormseed

As with many of the most ancient and popular herbs, epazote grows like a weed in the right conditions. It is a (tender) perennial in warm climates, but best treated as an annual in temperate areas. Epazote is reputed to have anti-parasitic and insecticidal effects, hence 'wormseed' as a common name.

⚠ **Poisonous in excess***

Family Amaranthaceae
Height 1.25m/4ft
Spread 75cm/30in
Hardiness Zone 3

* Over-consumption can cause severe illness and even death; any consumption to be avoided by pregnant women. Potential skin allergen. Use is legally restricted in some countries.

HOW TO USE

A herb well-known in its native Mexico for the ability of its leaves to enliven any number of dishes from soups and salads to pulses, epazote is also an essential ingredient for an authentic salsa. Consume only a little at a time; it is so pungent that a little goes a long way, in any case.

HOW TO GROW

Soak seeds overnight to speed up germination. Grow in rich, well-drained soil in full sun. Pinch out the tips, to encourage bushy growth. Remove dead plants in autumn.

HOW TO HARVEST

Pick leaves as required.

PUNGENT AUTHENTICITY

For the best salsas and quesadillas, substitute epazote for some or all of the coriander leaves – but use it very sparingly.

PERENNIAL

Cardamom
Elettaria cardamomum

Cardamom's powerfully aromatic seeds have a wide range of uses, but once extracted from the fruit and ground, they will quickly lose their fragrance. The plants originate from a rainforest habitat, and unless given near-perfect conditions are unfortunately unlikely to flower and fruit.

Family Zingiberaceae
Height 3m/10ft
Spread 3m/10ft
Hardiness Zone 1c

HOW TO USE
Seeds have a wide range of medicinal and culinary applications. They can sweeten both the breath (when chewed directly) and baked goods (as a ground spice), and they can flavour curries and other savoury ingredients, sweet and savoury preserves and drinks.

HOW TO GROW
Grow in rich, moist soil in dappled shade with plenty of heat and humidity year-round: seeds will germinate only at a minimum of 19°C/66°F.

HOW TO HARVEST
Pick fruits when ripe and dry them whole. Seeds can be extracted and ground as needed from the dried, stored fruits.

PRICEY SPICE
Cardamom must be harvested by hand, so is among the most expensive spices by weight in the world, along with saffron (see page 59) and vanilla, for example.

GROWING HERBS

PERENNIAL

Wasabi

Eutrema japonicum aka wasabia

Wasabi paste as sold in the shops is often doctored with, or made entirely from, horseradish (see page 37), so if you want to have the true Japanese ingredient it is easier to grow it yourself. Although in the wild wasabi prefers the banks of mountain streams and fresh running water, it can be grown in free-draining soil provided that it has access to enough water.

Family Brassicaceae
Height 40cm/16in
Spread 20cm/8in
Hardiness Zone 7

HOW TO USE
Traditionally, wasabi has been used as an antidote to fish poisoning, explaining its common accompaniment of sashimi (raw fish). The root is enjoyed when grated or as a paste, or is mixed with other ingredients as a dip. Flowers can be pickled with the leaves (*wasabi-zuke*), while fresh leaves can be used to wrap fish being steamed.

HOW TO GROW
Plant the tubers in free-draining but damp soil in partial shade, or in clear, running spring water if possible.

HOW TO HARVEST
Leaves and flowers can be picked as required. Roots are best dug up in autumn, eighteen months after planting.

EVERY CLOUD
The silver lining for wasabi growers is that the plants prefer a cloudy, temperate summer to a sunny, hot one. For the best harvests, replicate its native Japanese shady mountain-stream habitat.

WASABI

PROJECT 5

Harvesting seed and fennel pollen

Many herbs produce seeds that are just as tasty and invaluable as the leaves and so, when growing herbs, it pays to be able to harvest the seed crop too. Seeds can also be saved from flowering herbs to sow in order to create new plants – this is especially helpful and economical for annual plants.

Fennel (*Foeniculum vulgare*) pollen, deservedly popular on Michelin-starred plates of food and incredibly expensive to buy, is very easy to gather from home-grown plants following the same principles as harvesting seed by the cut-stalk method (see below). Wait until most of the individual flowers on the flower heads are open before cutting their stalks – it should be possible to see the yellow pollen grains on the flowers.

Always harvest seed and pollen on a dry, preferably sunny day.

THE ON-THE-PLANT METHOD
If there is some uncertainty about when the seeds will ripen, place a paper bag over the top of each seed head. Tie securely to each stalk so that no falling seeds can escape and leave them for a week or two. Shake the stalks occasionally; if the seeds have ripened and fallen, they will rattle around in the bag. Cut the stalks from the plant and then hang to ripen and dry further, as in the cut-stalk method (see below).

THE CUT-STALK METHOD
Cut seed- or flower heads with stalks long enough to protrude several centimetres from the paper bag. Upend the seed- or flower heads into the bag – it may be possible to fit several into one paper bag, but for the most efficient drying do not overcrowd them. Tie the bag around the stalks, leaving enough string to tie or hook up the bag somewhere cool and dry. After two weeks or so, give the stalks a shake – ripe seeds should have fallen to the bottom of the bag and be rattling around. Pollen will not be audible and will require a visual check. Shake the stalks again to make sure all the seed or pollen has been dislodged, then discard the seed or flower heads.

STORAGE
Tip the seed or pollen from the bag into a clean, dry jar and seal to store for up to a year. If there is a lot of chaff, tip the contents of the bag on to a clean, dry plate and sort out the seeds or pollen by hand – a painstaking, but therapeutic process.

1. On a dry day, select some good-quality fennel flower or seed heads.
2. Cut each head with plenty of stalk attached and upend it into a paper bag (never use a plastic one, because it would foster humidity and therefore rot).
3. Hang each bag somewhere cool and dry for about two weeks.
4. Then use fennel pollen or seed as needed.

HARVESTING SEED AND FENNEL POLLEN

HERBACEOUS PERENNIAL

Fennel

Foeniculum vulgare aka herb fennel, common fennel

All parts of this tall, feathery plant, which adds height and interest to a herb garden or ornamental border, can be used for its aniseed flavour. It should not to be confused with bulb or Florence fennel (*F. vulgare* var. *dulce*).

Family Apiaceae
Height 2m/7ft
Spread 50cm/20in
Hardiness Zone 5

HOW TO USE
Leaves can be added to salads or used as a garnish, while leaf bases can be cooked as vegetables or eaten raw. Dried stems make good skewers for fish. Pollen can be sprinkled over sweet or savoury dishes. Seeds are used whole or ground to flavour baked goods, sausages and liqueurs such as Sambuca, as well as to make tea.

HOW TO GROW
Fennel grows in most soils and positions, but prefers full sun and well-drained soil. It happily self-sows around the garden unless prevented by deadheading. Cut back dead stems in autumn or winter.

HOW TO HARVEST
Cut leaves and stems as required; leaf bases are at their most tender in spring. Harvest pollen and seed just before they are ready (see also page 68).

BRONZE FENNEL
The bronze version of fennel, *F. vulgare* 'Purpureum', is a stalwart of RHS Chelsea Flower Show gardens for its attractive foliage. It is edible, too, and good in a hot-coloured border.

HERBACEOUS PERENNIAL

Sweet woodruff

Galium odoratum aka bedstraw, kiss-me-quick

A mat-forming perennial that thrives in partial shade, sweet woodruff is ideal for ground cover or planting under shrubs and trees. The name derives from the Greek *gala*, meaning 'milk', referring to its historical use in curdling milk for cheese-making.

⚠ **Poisonous in excess***
Family Rubiaceae
Height 30cm/12in
Spread 1m/39in+
Hardiness Zone 7

HOW TO USE
Sprigs of foliage can be infused in white wine to make the traditional German May Day drink *Maibowle* or be used to decorate and add flavour to fruit cups. Flowers can be dried and used for their fragrance.

HOW TO GROW
Plant in moist but well-drained soil in partial shade. Sweet woodruff spreads almost infinitely when given good conditions.

HOW TO HARVEST
Pick foliage and flower sprigs as required.

SLEEP ON IT
To enable sweet woodruff to scent linen, put sachets of dried flowers between sheets and bedding when they are in storage.

SWEET WOODRUFF

PERENNIAL CLIMBER

Hop
Humulus lupulus aka hop vine

The southern English counties, particularly Kent, are strewn with eye-catching oast houses – barns specifically designed for the drying of the large hop harvests in this region. These days the harvests are more commercialized, and production occurs on much larger premises.

⚠ Skin irritant and potential allergen

Family Cannabaceae
Height 6m/20ft
Spread 50cm/20in
Hardiness Zone 6

HOW TO USE
The flowers are used to flavour and preserve beer, and also have a powerful sedative effect: once dried they can be stuffed into 'sleep pillows'. Whole 'bines' – the entire plant cut at the base and dried – make attractive decorations, while the young shoots can be cooked like asparagus.

HOW TO GROW
Cultivate in moist, rich soil in full sun or partial shade. Being a vigorous climber, the hop needs a sturdy support, such as a trellis, pergola or extensive wires. Wayward stems, especially the early shoots, may need training into the support. Cut back the dead growth and check the support in autumn or winter.

HOW TO HARVEST
Cut young shoots in spring. Gather flowers and bines in autumn, and hang to dry.

HIP HOPS
Microbreweries and craft beer producers, which are experimenting with hop varieties to produce flavourful beers, are fuelling a boom in hop-growing, particularly in the USA.

GROWING HERBS

PERENNIAL OR SHRUB

Hyssop
Hyssopus officinalis

A semi-evergreen perennial or shrub, hyssop develops into an appealing, informal, low hedge. For white flowers, choose *H. officinalis* f. *albus* or *H.o.* 'Roseus' for pink flowers.

HOW TO USE
Hyssop leaves are excellent when cooked, as they have a strong mint/rosemary/sage flavour with hints of citrus. Whether used as a component of a bouquet garni or on its own, hyssop will complement most meat and fish dishes, as well as soups and stews. It can also be infused into a sugar syrup for fruit dishes, and is traditionally added to fruit pies (especially cranberry) in North America. Dried leaves can be infused to make tea.

HOW TO GROW
Grow in well-drained soil in full sun. Trim hedges to shape and cut single plants back hard in spring, to promote fresh growth. Trim all plants after flowering.

HOW TO HARVEST
Pick leaves and enjoy fresh or dry, as required.

⚠ Avoid in pregnancy. The essential oil can cause fitting and is subject to legal restrictions in some countries.

Family Lamiaceae
Height 60cm/24in
Spread 90cm/36in
Hardiness Zone 7

CLEANSING HERB
Like many herbs, hyssop is an ancient plant. It is referred to in the Bible (Psalm 51:7 and other places) as having cleansing properties: 'Cleanse me with hyssop, and I shall be clean.'

TREE

Bay
Laurus nobilis aka bay tree, bay laurel

Bay was revered in both ancient Greek and Roman cultures, giving rise to its reputation as a mark of excellence: leaves were worn as crowns by athletes and politicians, and the 'laureate' title (as in Poet or Nobel) derives from this, too. *Laurus* itself is from *laudare*, the Latin 'to praise', and *nobilis* is Latin for 'noble'.

Family Lauraceae
Height 15m/50ft
Spread 10m/33ft
Hardiness Zone 4

HOW TO USE
Leaves, whether fresh or dried, are used to infuse all manner of savoury dishes and also fruit and cream desserts; they are rarely eaten by themselves. Bay is a main constituent of a bouquet garni, too.

HOW TO GROW
Although bay can develop into a large tree, it is easily contained and clipped into smaller specimens. It prefers well-drained soil and full sun, although it also thrives in partial shade. Prune in spring to maintain shape; bay can also be grown as a standard (see also Topiary herbs, page 110).

HOW TO HARVEST
Pick leaves as required: as it is evergreen, fresh leaves can be harvested year-round.
Cut stems to dry if required.

KEEP AT BAY
In Greek mythology, the gods turned Daphne into a bay tree to protect her from Apollo's unwanted advances; Culpeper wrote that bay will help the body to resist witchcraft.

GROWING HERBS

SHRUB

English lavender

Lavandula angustifolia aka lavender, common lavender

So common is it as a herb and ornamental plant that lavender needs no introduction. Take care to plant English lavender (*L. angustifolia*) for culinary use; French or butterfly lavender (*L. stoechas*) can be used for its fragrance but is poisonous to eat.

Family Lamiaceae
Height 1m/39in
Spread 1m/39in
Hardiness Zone 5

HOW TO USE
Use fresh or dried flower buds for perfume and to decorate baked goods and cocktails (see also Herbs for cocktails, page 104); leaves and non-flowering sprigs can be used to infuse sweet and savoury dishes (it is excellent with roast lamb). Dried flowers are also excellent in sachets, to perfume linen and deter clothes moths, and in relaxing pillows. Oil distilled from the flowers is a popular component of perfume and toiletries.

HOW TO GROW
Lavender prefers well-drained soil in full sun. The richer and moister the soil, the bushier the plant will be, but at a cost to the intensity of the oil in the leaves and flowers. Cut back after flowering to just above where the brown stem turns green.

HOW TO HARVEST
Cut flower stalks as the buds are just beginning to open; use fresh or hang upside down in bunches to dry, then rub off the dried buds to store.

LAVENDER SPECIES AND CULTIVARS
Compact plants suitable for hedging are *L. angustifolia* 'Hidcote', *L.a.* 'Imperial Gem' and *L.a.* 'Munstead'. White-flowered lavenders include *L.a.* 'Nana Alba' and a good pink cultivar is *L.a.* 'Lodden Pink'; of the other *L. angustifolia* cultivars there are most colours along the blue-purple spectrum with little variation in fragrance. For perfume, lavandin (*L.* x *intermedia*) is the form most used commercially; it has longer flower spikes and a more intense scent. *L. stoechas* and *L. dentata* are both less hardy than English lavender and lavandin and are used purely for ornament.

PROJECT 6

Drying herbs

Although with many herbs the fresh leaves give the best flavour or fragrance, dried home-grown herbs can be a good substitute, especially in winter months when fresh herbs are unavailable or in short supply.

DRYING HERBS: GENERAL PRINCIPLES
- Always gather the herbs on a dry, preferably sunny day so that the plants are already dry on the surface.
- Hang flowering stems upside down, so the stalks dry when they are straight rather than drooping over with the weight of the flower heads.
- Hang herbs in small bunches with sufficient space between them to allow for air circulation.
- Hang them to dry in a cool, dry place.
- Do not store herbs until they are completely dry – any moisture left in the herbs could encourage them to rot once sealed in a container.
- Store dried herbs in an airtight jar or tin, to maintain freshness, and use them within a year.

SOME WAYS TO DRY HERBS
All the culinary stalwarts are good candidates for drying: thyme, sage, oregano and rosemary. Once dry they can be chopped (ready to sprinkle into sauces and other dishes) before storing either individually or as dried mixed herbs. The herbes de Provence mix varies by producer, but typically contains rosemary, thyme, marjoram or oregano and savory.
- Oregano can be cut by the stem when the flowers are just starting to open; they can then be dried and stored as whole stems from which the flowers and leaves can be rubbed off into dishes.
- To dry English lavender for use in floral arrangements or the kitchen, cut the stems when the first buds have just opened; once dry they can be used as cut flowers or the buds rubbed off and stored in a jar for culinary purposes or for moth-repelling sachets.
- Bunches of mixed herbs can be used as bouquet garnis in stews and casseroles, or as fragrant firelighters.

1. Gather good-quality leaves and flowers on a dry day. Cut plenty of each stem to allow for space to tie the bunches together.
2. Tie the herbs in small bunches, using twine or natural string to allow for moisture to escape from under the tie.
3. Hang the bunches of herbs in a cool, dry place until they are completely desiccated.
4. Rub lavender buds off the stalks once they have dried.

DRYING HERBS

HERBACEOUS PERENNIAL

Lovage
Levisticum officinale aka love parsley, bladderseed

Historically used as a diuretic and an aphrodisiac, lovage is also a good plant for the back of the border. It is the only species in its genus.

⚠ Avoid during pregnancy

Family Apiaceae
Height 2m/7ft
Spread 1m/39in
Hardiness Zone 6

HOW TO USE
Lovage leaves can be infused into soups, stews and stocks, or stuffed into roasting joints. Stems can be blanched and eaten as a vegetable (they have a celery-like flavour) or candied. Seeds are added, sparingly, as a flavouring to bread and also soups and stews.

HOW TO GROW
Plant in rich, moist soil in full sun or partial shade. If the seed is not to be harvested, stems can be cut down after flowering, to promote fresh, leafy growth. Cut down again in autumn once the stems have died back.

HOW TO HARVEST
Pick fresh leaves as required. Cut stems in spring, when they are at their most tender. Collect seed as it ripens (see also page 68).

FEEL THE LOVE
In medieval times lovage was reputed to be an aphrodisiac, perhaps because of its deodorizing properties!

GROWING HERBS

HERBACEOUS PERENNIAL

Lemon balm
Melissa officinalis

This bushy, very forgiving plant to grow is also beloved by bees (which probably gave rise to its name: *melissa* is Greek for 'honey bee'). A lime version, *M. o.* 'Lime Balm', makes a similar-looking plant with furrier leaves and a distinct, citrus-lime scent.

Family Lamiaceae
Height 1m/39in
Spread 50cm/20in
Hardiness Zone 7

HOW TO USE
Fresh leaves can be enjoyed in salads, steeped to make tea and used in the production of Eau de Mélisse des Carmes Boyer (melissa cordial). Such leaves can also be infused in fruit cocktails. Dried leaves can be added to sleep pillows.

HOW TO GROW
Plant in moist, rich soil in full sun or partial shade. Cut back to the ground after flowering, for a fresh crop of leaves and to prevent widespread self-sowing. Cut down in autumn, once the stems have died back.

HOW TO HARVEST
Pick fresh leaves as required. For dry leaves, cut stems as flowering begins and hang up to dry.

PICK ME UP
Lemon balm is alleged to have a positive effect on low spirits, and is most commonly taken as a tea.

HERBACEOUS PERENNIAL

Mint
Mentha species

Family Lamiaceae
Height 1m/39in
Spread 50cm/20in
Hardiness Zone 7

Perhaps one of the most obvious herbs in everyday use, from the flavour of toothpaste to mint sauce with roast lamb, to teas and cocktails, it would not be an exaggeration to call the mint family indispensable. Species and cultivars demonstrate not only variation of the mint flavour itself, but also a range of added scents, from strawberry and chocolate to ginger.

HOW TO USE
Fresh leaves are added as a flavouring to any number of sweet and savoury dishes and drinks. Oil distilled from the leaves is used as a flavouring for food, drinks and toiletries and as a fragrance for many more products. Some mints are reputed to aid digestion and alleviate stomach upsets, and mint tea (made from fresh or dried leaves) has long been used as a digestif.

HOW TO GROW
Plant in moist, rich soil in partial shade or full sun. Mint spreads quickly using creeping stolons (overground roots) and unless monitored can quickly become invasive. Planting in a large pot, container or a dedicated raised bed can be a good solution. Cut back to the ground after flowering, for a fresh crop of leaves, then cut down in autumn once the stems have died back.

HOW TO HARVEST
Pick fresh leaves as required. Small portions of the plant can be potted up to overwinter indoors on a sunny windowsill and keep the supply of fresh leaves going until spring. Cut stems just before flowering and hang up to dry.

HERBACEOUS PERENNIAL

NOTABLE SPECIES AND CULTIVARS
Many of the 'flavoured' mints will be labelled only as their particular flavour: for example, 'Ginger Mint'. Be sure to check the leaves' smell and taste are as advertised, before buying.

M. × gracilis (Scotch mint)
Smooth leaves and red-tinged stems. A basil-tinged aroma and a warmer taste than some of the other mint species. Good with tomatoes and fruit.

M. × piperita (peppermint)
The main mint used for medicinal properties, it has purple-tinged leaves and dark purple stems and is the most soothing for the digestion.

MINT 81

HERBACEOUS PERENNIAL

M. × piperita f. citrata 'Basil'
Most of the 'flavoured' mints fall under M. × piperita f. citrata. As well as one with basil-scented leaves, other forms worth seeking out include 'Chocolate' and 'Lemon'.

M. × piperita f. citrata 'Variegata'
One of the two main variegated forms of mint (the other being M. × gracilis 'Variegata'), this plant has dark green-and-cream variegated leaves.

M. pulegium (pennyroyal)
A low-growing, creeping plant that was historically used to purify the water taken on long sea voyages. Leaves are added to pork products including black pudding and sausages and, when dried, can be used

MINT – A 'VERY PROFITABLE' HERB
Even Culpeper was quick to note that mint 'once planted in a garden, will hardly be rid out again'. However, this was compensated for by its many traditional uses, including helping against the 'biting of a mad dog' when applied with salt. He notes mint's soothing effect on the digestion: 'Briefly it is very profitable to the stomach.' However, that was about spearmint (M. spicata). Of wild or horsemint (probably M. longifolia), Culpeper writes that it is 'extremely bad for wounded people; and they say a wounded man that eats Mint, his wound will never be cured, and that is a long day'.

HERBACEOUS PERENNIAL

to deter mice and insects.

M. requienii (Corsican mint or rock mint)
This tiny plant grows no more than 1cm/½in high and forms a dense, spreading mat.

M. spicata (spearmint or garden mint)
Use this plant for mint sauce. It is also the mint most commonly infused in juleps and mojitos, with the cultivar 'Kentucky Colonel' being the traditional choice in the United States.

M. spicata var. *crispa* 'Moroccan'
For the most intense and best-flavoured mint tea, Moroccan mint is the only one to plant. Its leaves are set densely on the stems, so that only a short sprig is needed for each cup.

M. 'Strawberry Mint'
This plant is still known under various names and may also be advertised as *M.* × *piperita* 'Strawberry'. It is more delicate than other cultivars and has a distinct strawberry scent to its pale green leaves.

M. suaveolens (apple mint, woolly mint)
One of the best mints for cut-flower arrangements – the pale, furry leaves are borne on tall stems. The variegated form is also known as pineapple mint, for its fruity, sweet fragrance.

PROJECT 7

Herbs as a green roof

Green roofs are a brilliant way of bringing plants and wildlife to an urban area as well as having a number of benefits for the actual building, such as improved insulation and reduced rain run-off. While an extensive green roof requires significant planning and a number of structural considerations that can be best dealt with by expert companies, a smaller project such as a garden office roof or shed roof are achievable with a bit of DIY. Furthermore, the planting scheme can incorporate herbs for fragrance and (if they are within reach) consumption.

This is a basic introduction to the concept of a green roof and will supply some planting inspiration: for more detailed technical advice on constructing a green roof, consult specific books or experts on the subject.

A small green roof capable of supporting herb plants needs a rooting space of at least 10cm/4in – up to 20cm/8in if possible. This can be created using a grid or honeycomb lattice of plastic bars (or wood, but this will rot eventually, is heavier of itself and holds water weight). The resulting pockets of space can then be filled with compost and plants. Beneath the rooting medium there must be barriers to water ingress and also root penetration, as well as a filtering and drainage layer to prevent the potting compost from becoming waterlogged, which has the potential to kill the plants.

Whichever plants are used on a green roof, it will become a welcome habitat for insects and an invaluable resource for birds as well. Flowering species provide important nectar for pollinating and other insects such as bees, butterflies and hoverflies. Drought-tolerant plants are best: those suitable for sun or shade depending on the position of the roof. Depending on the plants selected, maintenance is minimal: cutting back once or twice a year to remove old stems and flower spikes of taller species. If access could be a problem, choose plants that need the least or no attention.

HERB PLANTS SUITABLE FOR A GREEN ROOF
Camomile (*Chamaemelum nobile*)
Chives (*Allium schoenoprasum*)
Creeping rosemary (*Salvia rosmarinus* Prostratus Group); where deep planting pockets are possible
English lavender (*Lavandula angustifolia*); use compact varieties such as 'Hidcote' and 'Nana Alba' where deeper planting pockets are possible
English mace (*Achillea ageratum*)
Oregano (*Origanum vulgare*); compact or creeping forms
Thyme (*Thymus* species); all species are ideal, in fact a purely thyme roof would be an excellent choice

HERBACEOUS PERENNIAL

Bergamot
Monarda didyma aka bee balm, monarda

Not to be confused with citrus bergamot (see page 56), which has a similar aroma, monarda is more commonly planted in ornamental borders. Different hybrids offer whorled flowers in generally bright colours including shades of red, pink and purple, but the true form of *M. didyma* bears scarlet flowers.

Family Lamiaceae
Height 1.25m/4ft
Spread 50cm/20in
Hardiness Zone 5

HOW TO USE
Fresh or dried leaves are added to drinks, including tea and iced ones; in tea they provide an Earl Grey-type flavour. Fresh flowers can be used as edible decorations and in salads.

HOW TO GROW
Grow in full sun and rich, moist soil. Dry conditions can easily lead to mildew on the leaves. Cut back the dead stems in autumn or in late winter.

HOW TO HARVEST
Pick fresh leaves and flowers as required. For leaves to dry, cut and hang stems before flowering. For dried flowers, cut and hang stems once the flowers are in full bloom.

SWEET NECTAR
Bergamot is a great food plant for pollinating insects – hence its common name, bee balm.

GROWING HERBS

TREE

Nutmeg
Myristica fragrans aka mace, jatiphala

These tropical trees are an important crop for countries such as Sri Lanka and Indonesia, but are so large as to be unlikely fruiting house plants in temperate climates. However, their fragrant, evergreen leaves and bushy habits make them attractive as smaller specimens.

⚠ **Poisonous in excess**
Family Myristicaceae
Height 20m/66ft
Spread 8m/26ft
Hardiness Zone 1a

HOW TO USE
Nutmeg is a widely enjoyed culinary spice, adding flavour to sweet and savoury dishes. It is particularly good with spinach and in cream sauces. Mace is generally used whole to infuse dishes with a more subtle nutmeg flavour. Both are used in ras-el-hanout. Consumption of either spice in excess can cause hallucinations and – in vast amounts – poisoning.

HOW TO GROW
The nutmeg tree grows best in free-draining, sandy but rich soil, in a very humid and warm atmosphere. Specimens grown indoors could be pruned to keep them to size.

HOW TO HARVEST
Fruits split open when ripe; remove the aril (mace) and seed (nutmeg) and allow to dry completely before storing.

NUTMEG AND MACE
This tree actually provides a double crop for its cultivators. The golden fruits ripen and split open to reveal the mace, a red covering (aril), which surrounds the brown nutmeg itself. Although the flavour of the two spices is similar, the concentration – and hence the pungency – of the essential oils within them varies. The fleshy part of the fruit is used to make fruity jellies or syrups and can also be candied and pickled.

NUTMEG 87

HERBACEOUS PERENNIAL

Sweet Cicely

Myrrhis odorata aka anise, garden myrrh, sweet chervil

The only species in its genus, sweet Cicely has historical uses as varied as a preventative measure against the plague to being an ingredient of furniture polish. It lives up to its common name of 'sweet' and can be enjoyed as a partial sugar substitute for fruit dishes, especially rhubarb whose first stems emerge at the same time as the new leaves of sweet Cicely, in early spring.

Family Apiaceae
Height 1.5m/5ft
Spread 1m/39in
Hardiness Zone 5

HOW TO USE
Leaves can be added raw to salads or cooked with fruit or savoury dishes, to which they add sweetness and a mild aniseed flavour. Cooked roots can be eaten either warm or cold, or be used to make wine. Seeds can be eaten unripe in desserts, salads or stir-fries; once ripe they can be enjoyed dry in spice rubs and baked goods.

HOW TO GROW
Rich, moist soil that is deep enough to accommodate a long taproot suits sweet Cicely, in partial or even full shade. Cut back after flowering, to stimulate a fresh crop of leaves. Then cut back all the foliage in autumn or late winter, once it has died back.

HOW TO HARVEST
Pick fresh leaves as required; they can also be dried to use when no fresh ones are available. Unripe seeds are green; they turn dark brown once ripe. Dig up roots in autumn, leaving some to re-sprout the following spring.

SWEET CRUMBLE
To use sweet Cicely in a rhubarb crumble, finely chop the leaves and add to the fruit base, using the same volume of leaves as for the sugar.

SHRUB

Myrtle
Myrtus communis

Myrtle makes an attractive hedge or specimen shrub, and while it does not like cold and wet conditions (it originates in the Mediterranean) it does tolerate coastal climates. There are variegated and dwarf forms as well as double-flowered varieties.

Family Myrtaceae
Height 2.5m/8ft
Spread 2.5m/8ft
Hardiness Zone 4

HOW TO USE
This herb is suitable for robust flavours such as red meat and game dishes, especially when cooked on an open fire or barbecue: use the leaves or dry berries (as a spice rub). The latter substitute well for juniper. Myrtle is also used to make myrtle liqueur.

HOW TO GROW
Grow myrtle in full sun and well-drained soil: wet soil in winter reduces its chances of surviving low temperatures. Trim in spring to remove any foliage that died back over winter, to stimulate fresh growth and to re-shape if required.

HOW TO HARVEST
Pick fresh leaves as required, but not too heavily over winter. Gather leaves for drying or preserving in oil, in midsummer. Berries are ripe when purple-black; dry them in a warm, dry place such as an airing cupboard or sunny windowsill. Store in an airtight container.

QUEEN'S FAVOURITE
Closely related *Ugni molinae* (syn. *Ugni molinae*) bears berries – known as Chilean guava – that were the preferred fruit of Queen Victoria.

MYRTLE 89

ANNUAL OR PERENNIAL

Basil
Ocimum species aka garden basil, sweet basil

Family Lamiaceae
Height 30–60cm/12–24in
Spread 20–30cm /8–12in
Hardiness Zone 1b

Although basil is commonly associated with Italian cooking, it actually originates from Asia and Africa. Its essential oils are many and varied, and include anise, rose, thyme and clove, with individual cultivars drawing out some scents such as cinnamon or lemon more than others. The aroma of basil is arguably better than the taste, and capturing its elusive nature is difficult: the chef Heston Blumenthal once devised a basil spray to mist the air around diners as they ate a pizza, finding this preferable to serving the leaves on the dish itself.

HOW TO USE
Generally only the leaves are used, and they are best raw or added at the last minute to cooked dishes, to preserve their unique flavour and fragrance. Basil is the most common constituent of the sauce pesto, and its leaves are also added to many Italian dishes of pasta, salads and pizza. Flowers can decorate savoury and sweet dishes. The plants have some religious connotations too; basil is grown widely in Hindu cultures for its protective influence on temples and the home. More prosaically, the branches can be hung to repel insects such as mosquitoes.

HOW TO GROW
The plants require heat and plenty of sun to thrive, and in cool-temperate climates are better grown under cover or on a sunny windowsill. They prefer light, free-draining soil. The annual species (most culinary basils) require re-sowing every year; discard old plants. Tender perennials such as 'African Blue' can be overwintered in a heated greenhouse or in the form of cuttings. All plants can be encouraged into bushier growth by regularly pinching out the growing tips.

HOW TO HARVEST
Pick fresh leaves and flowers as required.

ANNUAL OR PERENNIAL

NOTABLE SPECIES AND CULTIVARS
O. 'African Blue'
Although the purple-green leaves have a distinct basil fragrance, this tender perennial is best used as an ornamental. It has purple stems and spikes of purple-blue flowers from mid- to late summer.

O. basilicum
The most widely grown and known of the basil species, sweet or garden basils are annuals with mid-green leaves and spikes of white flowers borne from mid- to late summer. *O. basilicum* 'Genovese' is traditionally used for pesto; 'Napolitano' (syn. 'Lettuce Leaf') bears larger, crinkled leaves; 'Purple Ruffles' is a more ornamental basil with crinkled leaf margins; 'Siam Queen' is a good choice for Thai dishes and produces a more aniseed or liquorice aroma. Other cultivars are sold simply as types, for example, cinnamon basil; test the leaves first to ensure the scent is as the label suggests.

O. × *citriodorum* (lemon basil)
This annual has thinner leaves than *O. basilicum* and a good citrus scent that pairs well with fish and chicken dishes. The seeds can also be infused in water as a tonic drink.

O. minimum (Greek basil)
The most compact of all basil plants, with short, bushy stems and small leaves with a powerful scent. An annual.

SOWING PROFANITIES
In ancient Mediterranean cultures it was believed that cursing while sowing basil seeds would improve germination rates.

BASIL

SUBSHRUB

Marjoram
Origanum marjorana aka sweet marjoram

Closely related to – and easily confused with – oregano (*O. vulgare*; see opposite), marjoram is less robust both in growth and in flavour than its cousin. In colder climates it can be grown as an annual for its warm, sweet, thyme-like aroma, or be overwintered in a pot under cover of a greenhouse.

Family Lamiaceae
Height 60cm/24in
Spread 45cm/18in
Hardiness Zone 4

HOW TO USE
Leaves and flowers (often as sprigs rather than individual blooms) can be added to meat, fish and tomato dishes, preferably towards the end of cooking to best preserve their flavour. Sprigs can also flavour oils and vinegars (see also Herb oils, vinegars, spirits and waters, page 40).

HOW TO GROW
Marjoram prefers well-drained, even dry, soil (it dislikes wet soil over winter) and a position in full sun. Cut back stems after flowering, to stimulate fresh leafy growth. Prune again in early spring, to remove weak or dead growth and keep this perennial to size.

HOW TO HARVEST
Pick fresh leaves and flowering sprigs as required.

FRESH NOT DRY
Marjoram's more delicate flavour means it is better when used fresh, whereas oregano is more suitable for drying.

PERENNIAL

Oregano
Origanum vulgare aka wild marjoram

Family Lamiaceae
Height 1m/39in
Spread 1m/39in
Hardiness Zone 6

Oregano further confuses the oregano or marjoram (see opposite) identification process by taking various forms depending on its situation. In general, it is a bushy plant, with upright (but sometimes spreading) stems that bear beautiful, purple-pink flowers in summer.

HOW TO USE
The leaves can be added to soups, stews and roasting meats; they also pair well with any dish that includes garlic, chilli or tomatoes. Oregano's robust flavour suits winter and autumn dishes better than summer ones, although the fresh leaves can be added sparingly to salads and pizzas. Leaves and flowering sprigs can be infused for tea or in oils and vinegars. The powerful oil is used commercially as a flavouring and in toiletries (particularly men's fragrances).

HOW TO GROW
This herb grows best in warm, sunny spot with well-drained to dry soil. Cut back stems once flowering has finished, to stimulate fresh leaves.

HOW TO HARVEST
Pick fresh leaves and flowering sprigs as required. Stems can be cut just before flowers open and hung to dry, for use in winter months.

MOUNTAIN BEAUTY
Oregano derives from the Greek for mountain (*oros*), which is indicative of its preferred habitat, and the Greek for joy or beauty (*ganos*).

PROJECT 8

Hey pesto!

Easily the most well-known of all herbal sauces, pesto has become a store-cupboard staple. This has its downsides though, as the connection with the original ingredients can be lost, especially with some retailers now labelling their basic basil version as simply 'green pesto'. However, even the most expensive jar from the deli cannot compete with a home-made sauce using fresh-picked herbs.

Traditionally, pesto would be made with basil, and the variety 'Genovese' specifically, but actually any number of herb and nut combinations can be used. For a robust winter pesto, try parsley instead of basil and walnuts or hazelnuts instead of pine nuts. Chives or wild garlic also make excellent variations.

This pesto recipe makes *c.*220g/8oz.

INGREDIENTS
25g/1oz pine nuts
100g/3½oz fresh basil leaves
1 garlic clove, crushed
½ lemon, rind
50–100ml/1½–3½fl oz extra virgin olive oil
50g/2oz Parmesan cheese, finely grated
Salt and pepper to taste

METHOD
Toast the nuts in a dry frying pan over a medium heat until aromatic, moving them constantly (this will take five minutes or less). Place the nuts with the basil leaves, garlic and lemon rind into a food processor and pulse until the leaves are finely chopped. Add 50ml/2fl oz olive oil and blitz further to a paste. Stir in the Parmesan and then season to taste; add more oil to bring the pesto to the desired consistency if using immediately.

To use later: Pack into sterilized jars, then add olive oil to cover the top with a layer 5–10mm/¼–½in thick. This will help to preserve the pesto and keep it from browning. Add more oil over the top every time you take out some pesto. Store in the refrigerator and use within a month.

HEY PESTO!

ANNUAL

Poppy

Papaver rhoeas aka corn poppy, field poppy

The seeds of the iconic red poppy of cornfields and also of the First World War lie dormant in the soil for many years, germinating in freshly turned soil. If grown with or near other annual poppies, such as the opium poppy (*P. somniferum*, from which opium and morphine are derived), resulting seedlings can be of mixed colouring.

⚠ All parts except the seeds are toxic if ingested

Family Papaveraceae
Height 75cm/30in
Spread 20cm/8in
Hardiness Zone 7

HOW TO USE
The seeds can be used (as can those of *P. somniferum*) in baking breads and cakes and in savoury dishes. The fresh or dry seed heads are attractive in cut-flower displays.

HOW TO GROW
Poppies prefer well-drained soil in full sun. The final size of the plant varies depending on the conditions in which it is grown – the richer and moister the soil the larger the plant. Remove plants once they die back in autumn, and re-sow (or allow plants to self-sow) in spring.

HOW TO HARVEST
Harvest the seed heads using the cut-stalk method (see Harvesting seed and fennel pollen, page 68).

RESTRICTED GROWTH
The opium poppy's powerful constituents means it can be grown only under a pharmaceutical licence in some countries, so ensure your seeds have been correctly identified as *P. rhoeas* and not *P. somniferum*.

96 GROWING HERBS

PERENNIAL

Scented pelargonium
Pelargonium aka scented-leaf pelargonium

Sometimes incorrectly called geraniums, scented-leaf pelargoniums are a group of hybrid *Pelargonium*, related to the ornamental regal, zonal and ivy-leaved pelargoniums. All make good house plants in cool-temperate climates, or patio plants in warm seasons and warmer climates. There are many different scents, of which rose (for example, 'Attar of Roses'), lemon or citrus and mint are the most easily identifiable.

Family Geraniaceae
Height 50–100cm/20–39in
Spread 50–100cm/20–39In
Hardiness Zone 2

HOW TO USE
The intensely fragranced leaves can be used to infuse and scent sugars, and to flavour syrups, baked goods and other desserts. The essential oils are used commercially for perfumery and toiletries.

HOW TO GROW
Grow in pots of light compost or (where year-round temperatures permit) in well-drained soil. Plants prefer full sun, but tolerate some dappled shade. Deadhead as appropriate. Cut back to a short framework of stems in early spring, to keep plants to shape.

HOW TO HARVEST
Pick fresh leaves as required.

SCENTED WONDERS
Other fragrances of scented pelargoniums include woody, resinous or eucalyptus types, cinnamon, lavender, coconut, apple and chocolate.

SCENTED PELARGONIUM

ANNUAL

Shiso
Perilla frutescens aka beefsteak plant

A vigorous, bushy plant, shiso is an attractive summer bedding annual. Its leaves are used widely in Asian cooking and, although not distinctly sweet to taste, contain a chemical (perillaldehyde) that is 2,000 times sweeter than sugar.

Family	Lamiaceae
Height	1m/39in
Spread	60cm/24in
Hardiness	Zone 3

HOW TO USE
Fresh leaves can be enjoyed as a garnish or in salads, or used for wrapping meats before cooking. They can be substituted for basil to make pesto (see page 94), as well as be pickled. Flower spikes picked before the flowers open can be fried (as a vegetable). Dried seeds can be used as a condiment or sprouted for salads.

HOW TO GROW
Moist, rich soil in full sun is preferred, but shiso also tolerates partial shade. Pinch out the tips regularly, to encourage bushy growth. Remove dead plants in autumn, and re-sow in spring.

HOW TO HARVEST
Pick fresh leaves and flowers as required. Harvest seeds when ripe (see also Harvesting seed and fennel pollen, page 68).

HERBS AS BEDDING PLANTS
Shiso is increasingly being used as a summer annual in bedding schemes, where its vigorous nature ensures the ground is quickly covered with foliage. The purple, ruffle-leaved variant, *Perilla frutescens* var. *crispa*, is especially striking and is a good foil for red-, orange- and yellow-flowered plants. In a herb garden or pot, it could be combined with marigolds (*Calendula officinalis*), chillies (*Capsicum*) or nasturtiums (*Tropaeolum majus*) or be used to enhance the purple in borage flowers (*Borago officinalis*).

HERBACEOUS PERENNIAL

Asian mint

Persicaria odorata aka Vietnamese coriander, rau ram

Similar in appearance to other ornamental *Persicaria* species, this sprawling, spreading, tender perennial is alleged to have an anaphrodisiac effect. Its stems readily root where their joints touch the ground, so Asian mint is best contained in a pot that could also be brought under cover for protection from cold weather.

Family Polygonaceae
Height 45cm/18in
Spread 1.25m/4ft
Hardiness Zone 1c

HOW TO USE
Leaves vary in flavour depending on their age: young, fresh ones taste much like coriander (see page 58), while older leaves have a much hotter flavour. They can be added to salads, chicken and egg dishes.

HOW TO GROW
Rich, moist soil in full sun or partial shade is preferred; if growing it in a pot, keep the potting compost continually moist. Cut back spreading stems as necessary and prune out dead flower spikes after flowering.

HOW TO HARVEST
Pick fresh leaves as required.

HOT MINT
Asian mint is not really a mint at all, and is best treated as an annual and re-sown each spring if there's no space for its sprawling form indoors in winter.

ASIAN MINT

ANNUAL OR BIENNIAL

Parsley
Petroselinum crispum aka ache, devil-and-back-ten-times

One of parsley's unusual common names derives from the legend that the seeds, once sown, travel to hell and back ten times before they sprout – and since the Devil keeps some for himself on each visit one should sow ten times as much as is needed. These days germination rates are a little more reliable, and parsley is a stalwart of the herb garden and the kitchen. The species bears curly leaves; for flat leaves grow *P. crispum* var. *neapolitanum*.

Family Apiaceae
Height 50cm/20in
Spread 50cm/20in
Hardiness Zone 6

HOW TO USE
Fresh leaves can be added (sparingly) to salads, or chopped for gremolata, pesto (see page 94), salsa verde, tabbouleh, persillade and chimichurri. It is better than basil in *spaghetti alla puttanesca* (aka whore's spaghetti); leaves and stalks can be cooked in sauces and stews, and used to flavour stocks.

HOW TO GROW
Although a biennial, parsley is best treated as a hardy annual. Sow in succession from spring to late summer for a ready supply of fresh leaves year-round. Discard plants once they are tired, weak or more than a year old.

HOW TO HARVEST
Pick fresh leaves and stalks as required – plants will re-sprout several times after being cut.

BREATH FRESHENER
A leaf or two chewed on its own after a meal is believed to ease digestion and freshen the breath: 'And then, feeling rather sick, he went to look for some parsley' (*The Tale of Peter Rabbit*, Beatrix Potter).

GROWING HERBS

ANNUAL

Aniseed

Pimpinella anisum aka anise

Although many herbs have aniseed flavours, this is the true aniseed, which is used for the confectionery aniseed balls and in a number of liqueurs. Many umbel-flowered herbs look very similar so be sure that your plant is the true aniseed, as some other species are poisonous.

Family	Apiaceae
Height	50cm/20in
Spread	30cm/12in
Hardiness	Zone 3

HOW TO USE
The seeds are more widely enjoyed than the leaves, in baking, curries and to make drinks such as ouzo and pastis. The leaves can be added fresh to salads, and cooked in soups and vegetable dishes.

HOW TO GROW
Full sun and rich, sandy or well-drained soil suit aniseed best. For the seeds to ripen, the summer must be long and hot. Remove dead plants at the end of the growing season, and sow fresh the following spring.

HOW TO HARVEST
Pick fresh leaves as required. Harvest seed as it ripens (see also Harvesting seed and fennel pollen, page 68).

GARDEN WILDLIFE
Aniseed's strong smell and chemical components make it an effective insect repellent, but the fragrance will also attract mice and rats.

PERENNIAL

Pepper
Piper nigrum aka black pepper

Family	Piperaceae
Height	4m/13ft
Spread	20cm/8in
Hardiness	Zone 1a

Pepper is a ubiquitous spice in kitchens and on dining tables. Native to India, it grows as a vine that bears berries on short spikes. These are used in various ways: unripe fresh and pickled berries are green peppercorns, while unripe and dried they are black peppercorns. Berries picked ripe and retted (soaked in water for two weeks) can each have the inner seed – a white peppercorn – removed from the flesh.

HOW TO USE
Peppercorns – whole or ground – add spice and flavour to almost any savoury dish and many sweet ones.

HOW TO GROW
Dappled shade and high humidity, with rich, well-drained soil and tropical conditions, are best for this jungle plant. Its climbing shoots need strong supports or a frame. To promote fruiting, cut back stems to around 30cm/12in long, retaining and tying in the dozen strongest shoots, three or four times a year.

HOW TO HARVEST
Pick berries ripe or unripe as required.

PRICE OF PEPPER
Pepper was once so valuable it could be used as money (as in a 'peppercorn rent').

SHRUB

Rose
Rosa

Family Rosaceae
Height 1–1.5m/3–5ft
Spread 1–1.5m/3–5ft
Hardiness Zone 7

The two best rose selections for herbal uses are the rugosa or Japanese seaside rose (*Rosa rugosa*) and apothecary's rose (*R. gallica* var *officianlis*). Both have highly perfumed flowers and the rugosa rose has the largest, juiciest hips of all roses, so where there is room for only one plant, make it a rugosa rose. The species bears pink flowers and there is a white-flowered form (*R. rugosa* 'Alba'); bear in mind that the white flowers will not add any colour to infusions.

HOW TO USE
The flowers can infuse sugars, sugar syrups and alcohol with their scent and flavour. These, or the petals directly, can be added to desserts and baked goods. The hips can be made into jam, jelly or a syrup. Do not ingest the hips directly as they are full of tiny hairs that are an irritant to the throat.

HOW TO GROW
Cultivate in fertile soil in full sun or dappled shade. Rugosa roses can be grown as an informal hedge, spaced about 75cm/30in apart. Prune dead and older rugosa rose stems to the ground, to relieve congestion. Deadheading back to a healthy shoot and removing (in winter) any dead or congested growth is all the pruning the apothecary's rose needs.

HOW TO HARVEST
Cut flowers when they have just opened, for the best fragrance. Harvest hips once they are ripe and feel soft to a gentle squeeze.

FOR THE LOVE OF A ROSE
Roses have long symbolized love – the ubiquity of red roses in florist shops around Valentine's Day attests to that – and Shakespeare chose the flower of love for Juliet to bemoan Romeo's surname: 'What's in a name? That which we call a rose by any other word would smell as sweet.' However, it pays to heed the language of flowers when giving roses as a gift, for not all of them symbolize true love, as the red rose does. Almost all of the roses have favourable meanings attached, from grace (pink), modesty (pale peach) and fascination (orange) to enchantment (purple), but a yellow rose signifies infidelity or jealousy, so choose with care.

PROJECT 9

Herbs for cocktails

Nothing says summer like a refreshing cocktail (or mocktail), and home-grown herbs can add a little something extra to the flavour as well as the look of drinks, large and small. They can infuse alcohols, be steeped in syrups to then use as mixers, muddled (coarsely crushed) fresh into a glass or enjoyed simply as decorations – thus herbs can be as much a part of the drinks cupboard as the drinks themselves.

FLAVOURINGS FOR SPIRITS

Gin is the most obvious spirit to flavour with botanical elements, and it lends itself well to further enhancement with fresh herbs, but more neutral alcohols such as vodka can give a purer herb taste to the finished product. Sugar syrups steeped with herbs can also be used to mix with alcohols (pure or infused), to add another dimension to cocktails and are faster to make than infusing the alcohol. The following herbs are some of the best to infuse alcohol (see also Herb oils, vinegars, spirits and waters, page 40) or in a sugar syrup (see Infused sugar syrups, page 32). As with all cooking, experiment with favourite flavours or new varieties – try chocolate mint, lemon or orange thyme or pineapple sage, for example.

Basil (*Ocimum basilicum*)
Bay (*Laurus nobilis*)
Cardamom (*Elettaria cardamomum*)
Camomile (*Chamaemelum nobile*)
Chilli pepper (*Capsicum annuum*)
Citrus bergamot (*Citrus* × *limon* Bergamot Group)
Clove (*Syzygium aromaticum*)
Coriander (*Coriandrum sativum*)
Elderflower (*Sambucus nigra*)
Electric daisies (*Acmella oleracea*)
English lavender (*Lavandula angustifolia*)
Fennel (*Foeniculum vulgare*)
Horseradish (*Armoracia rusticana*)
Lemon verbena (*Aloysia citriodora*)
Mint (*Mentha* species)
Rose (*Rosa rugosa*)
Rosemary (*Salvia rosmarinus*, syn. *Rosmarinus officinalis*)
Saffron (*Crocus sativus*)
Scented pelargonium (*Pelargonium*)
Sweet Cicely (*Myrrhis ordorata*)
Sweet violet (*Viola odorata*)
Thyme (*Thymus* species)

MUDDLING HERBS

The most obvious muddled herb is mint, in the classic mojito, but pineapple sage (*Salvia elegans*), blackcurrant sage (*Salvia microphylla* var. *microphylla*), basil and lemon verbena are all good muddling herbs as well.

GARNISHES

Use sprigs of fresh herbs, especially flowering sprigs if available, to garnish a cocktail. Other edible flowers such as borage and scented pelargonium, nasturtium, marigold or electric daisies (for more adventurous guests) can be scattered over the top of a drink, or preserved in ice cubes.

MAKING FLOWER ICE CUBES
Put fresh flowers, petals or small sprigs of herbs into the compartments of an ice-cube tray and cover carefully with water. Prod down any parts of the flowers that are protruding above the water, and place in the freezer.

HERBS FOR COCKTAILS

HERBACEOUS PERENNIAL

Sorrel
Rumex acetosa

Family	Polygonaceae
Height	50cm/20in
Spread	10cm/4in
Hardiness	Zone 7

Although closely related to dock – that scourge of a weed – sorrel is worth planting for its lemon-flavoured young leaves. Regular picking ensures a supply in spring and early summer. Other types worth trying include buckler-leaved or French sorrel (*R. scutatus*) and attractive, red-veined sorrel (*R. sanguineus*).

HOW TO USE
Fresh, young leaves can be added to salads, to flavour and colour mayonnaise, and to new potatoes, egg and fish dishes (older leaves have a more bitter taste). Sorrel juice can be used as a cleaning agent.

HOW TO GROW
Cultivate this herb in moist soil in partial shade – the shade prevents the plant from flowering too soon in the season. Cut back after flowering, to stimulate a fresh crop of leaves. Remove all the dead foliage in autumn.

HOW TO HARVEST
Pick young leaves as required.

THIRST QUENCHING
Roman soldiers used to suck sorrel leaves to alleviate their thirst. The juice can also be used to curdle milk.

SHRUB OR PERENNIAL

Sage
Salvia species

Family	Lamiaceae
Height	75cm/30in
Spread	1m/39in
Hardiness	Zone 5

Native, like its culinary partners rosemary and thyme, to the Mediterranean region, sage has a powerful camphor scent that limits its culinary uses. Medicinally, a gargling tea or syrup can be made as a traditional home remedy for a sore throat, and when eaten sage is considered to aid digestion.

HOW TO USE
Sage is best introduced sparingly and with robust flavours in the kitchen. It pairs well with pork, apple, winter squash, pumpkin and beans. With onions, sage forms a traditional stuffing recipe, and its young leaves, particularly of clary sage (*S. sclarea*), can be battered and fried. The flower spikes of clary sage and annual clary (*S. viridis*) make good cut flowers, while those of *S. officinalis* are tasty when picked individually off the spikes and scattered over a salad. Commercially, sage oil is a component of some toiletries and a fixative for perfumes; clary sage and annual clary are used in the production of some wines, beers and liqueurs.

HOW TO GROW
Grow in well-drained soil in full sun or dappled shade. Cut back after flowering to maintain shape. Replace plants every five years or so, as they become woody and scrubby.

HOW TO HARVEST
Pick fresh leaves and flower spikes as required. Stems can be cut and hung up to dry.

SHRUB OR PERENNIAL

NOTABLE SPECIES AND CULTIVARS

S. elegans (pineapple sage)
This tender perennial (hardiness: zone 1c) bears bright green leaves with a distinct pineapple scent, as well as scarlet flowers. Fresh sprigs can be added to drinks and fresh fruit dishes.

S. officinalis
The main culinary sage, its soft, grey-green leaves are a perfect foil for the blue-purple flowers borne in midsummer.

S. officinalis 'Purpurascens' (purple sage)
An attractive stalwart in many herb gardens for its deep purple leaves, tinged with grey-green. It can be used in the same way as the species, and is actually preferred by some medicinal herbalists.

S. sclarea (clary sage)
This short-lived perennial or biennial produces spikes of striking, pink-and-cream flowers. It has a vanilla-balsam aroma.

S. viridis (annual clary, bluebeard)
An annual with bright green leaves and dark purple flowers. Historically used in snuff, it can be added as a flavouring to food and drinks but is also naturally antiseptic.

SHRUB

Rosemary
Salvia rosmarinus syn. *Rosmarinus officinalis*

Family	Lamiaceae
Height	2m/7ft
Spread	2m/7ft
Hardiness	Zone 4

Rosemary is a versatile shrub, both in the garden and the kitchen. Its flowers are an important nectar source for bees in early spring. For white flowers, grow the form *S. albiflorus* or 'Roseus' for pink flowers; 'Sissinghurst Blue' is more free-flowering than most other varieties and has a slightly more upright habit.

HOW TO USE
Rosemary's strong flavour is best imparted from the finely chopped leaves or from whole sprigs, which can be removed after roasting lamb and other meats. It is used in many other savoury dishes, especially with beans, sausages and stews, as well as in soups and some sweet foods. Rosemary can be infused in oils and vinegars, too; the oil is used commercially as a fragrance and in toiletries.

HOW TO GROW
Rosemary thrives in well-drained soil in full sun; it dislikes consistently wet soil in winter. Prune after flowering, to promote bushy growth and maintain shape.

HOW TO HARVEST
Cut fresh green sprigs as required and strip the leaves in the kitchen; do not over-pick young plants before they are able to get established. Cut longer, woody stems to use as skewers more sparingly – having several plants ensures a good supply; strip off the leaves before use.

ROASTING STICKS
Rosemary stems can be made into single-use skewers to impart flavour to meat or vegetables; cut each end to a point and strip off the leaves before skewering food.

PROJECT 10

Topiary herbs

Topiary – the practice of clipping plants into any shape ranging from a sphere or cone to a peacock or elephant – is a neat way of keeping a plant trained while adding interest to a garden. The formal structure in the shapes of these clipped plants provides relief for the eye among other, more billowing species. In a potager or herb garden, topiary can form focal points (a large standard bay in the centre of a bed, for example, with its lollipop of foliage atop a clear stem usually around 1m/39in high). It can also develop into low hedges, perhaps punctuated or cornered by larger cones or spheres. The use of these plants as edging and hedges dates back to the sixteenth century – the age of Elizabeth I – when they were used as fragrant components of knot gardens.

HERBS SUITABLE FOR TOPIARY

Popular plant choices to train as a standard include:

Bay (*Laurus nobilis*)
English lavender (*Lavandula angustifolia*)
Rosemary (*Salvia rosmarinus*, syn. *Rosmarinus officinalis*)

For plants grown in the ground or pots, the following herbs can be clipped into individual shapes or be trained as a hedge:

Bay (*Laurus nobilis*)
English lavender (*Lavandula angustifolia*)
Hyssop (*Hyssopus officinalis*)
Myrtle (*Myrtus communis*)
Rosemary (*Salvia rosmarinus*, syn. *Rosmarinus officinalis*)
Sage (*Salvia* species)

MAINTENANCE OF TOPIARY PLANTS

Ensure potted specimens are kept well-watered and fed throughout the growing season, and repot as necessary. Clip topiary shapes once or twice in summer, to keep them to shape.

1. Cut off side shoots of plants growing as standards (here, a bay tree) to keep a clear stem and limit regrowth there. Shoots from the base should be torn off as low as possible to hinder more growth.
2. When shaping the head, always prune to just above a node to avoid ugly dead stubs that are more susceptible to infection.
3. Ensure the head size is in balance with the clean stem.

TOPIARY HERBS 111

SHRUB OR TREE

Elder

Sambucus nigra aka elderflower, common elder

This large, branching shrub or small tree is a common plant in urban scrubland and rural hedges, thanks to birds distributing its seeds from the black berries. Modern cultivars, for example purple-leaved varieties, have similar uses to the species, but compare the potency of flower fragrance before choosing.

⚠ Leaves and raw berries are harmful if eaten

Family Adoxaceae
Height 6m/20ft
Spread 3m/10ft
Hardiness Zone 6

HOW TO USE
Flowers can be steeped to make cordial (also the main commercial use of the plant) and an alcoholic 'champagne' drink, as well as added as a flavouring in other drinks and fruit dishes and preserves (it pairs well with gooseberries, which ripen at the same time of year). When dried (see Drying herbs, page 76), the flowers can be used to make tea. Berries can be made into sauces, especially Pontack sauce, drinks such as elderberry rob, and other preserves. The leaves can be boiled and then strained to produce an insecticidal spray.

HOW TO GROW
Grow in rich, moist soil in full sun or partial shade. Elder can be kept to size by annual pruning in late winter and can be cut back as hard as necessary (it will easily grow 2m/7ft in one year).

HOW TO HARVEST
When foraging wild trees, be sure they are not close to roads or other dusty pollutants of the flowers. Leave some flowers to develop into fruits. Pick the flowers on a dry day when half the individual blooms on each flower head are open. Harvest berries when they have turned a deep purple-black. Leaves can be picked any time in summer, to use fresh in a spray.

GUARDIAN ELDER
Elder has many superstitions and legends associated with it, including that planting a specimen near the house is generally a protective measure.

GROWING HERBS

PERENNIAL

Salad burnet
Sanguisorba minor aka garden burnet

Salad burnet provides good edging for beds and borders – brushing against plants while walking or lightly crushing the leaves underfoot releases the cool fragrance. Although a culinary plant, this herb takes its genus name from the medicinal uses of a related species – *S. officinalis* – a literal translation from the Latin is 'to soak up blood' from *sanguis* ('blood') and *sorbere* ('to soak up').

Family	Rosaceae
Height	60cm/24in
Spread	30cm/12in
Hardiness	Zone 6

HOW TO USE
The leaves are enjoyed fresh when young, in salads and with soft cheese, having a cucumber-like taste. Older leaves are best infused in water or other drinks, or dried to make tea.

HOW TO GROW
Grow in moist to well-drained soil in dappled shade. Cut back after flowering, to stimulate the production of fresh leaves.

HOW TO HARVEST
Pick fresh leaves as required.

LAND GRABBER
Salad burnet has an extensive root system, which is useful in controlling land erosion and in reclaiming waste ground such as open mines.

ANNUAL

Summer savory
Satureja hortensis

This herb is a traditional flavouring for sausages in Germany and a component of herbes de Provence. Similar to oregano (see page 93) and thyme (see pages 124–7) in flavour, there is also a hint of pine in its flavour profile.

Family Lamiaceae
Height 20cm/8in
Spread 30cm/12in
Hardiness Zone 6

HOW TO USE
Summer savory leaves work well in most sauces, particularly tomato sauces, and with most vegetables. They can also be enjoyed in a marinade for olives and are a good flavouring for meat, fish and dairy dishes.

HOW TO GROW
Grow in well-drained – even dry – soil in full sun. Pinch out the tips of young shoots, to encourage bushy growth. Remove the plant once it has died in late autumn. New plants from seed sown in autumn can be overwintered in a heated greenhouse or indoors; or grow winter savory (see opposite) for supplies later in the season.

HOW TO HARVEST
Pick fresh leaves as required. Leafy stems can be cut and hung to dry.

GARDEN COMPANIONS
Summer savory may help as a companion plant in deterring blackfly from broad beans, and it is delicious cooked with the beans as well.

PERENNIAL

Winter savory
Satureja montana

Family Lamiaceae
Height 30cm/12in
Spread 30cm/12in
Hardiness Zone 5

A semi-evergreen plant, winter savory supplies much the same flavours as its summer cousin (see opposite), but can be picked year-round. The leaves have slightly more spice to them, and are stronger than summer savoury, so can be used more sparingly. For lemon-flavoured leaves, choose *S. montana* var. *citriodora*.

—

HOW TO USE
Leaves add a good flavour to soups and stews, meat, bean and vegetable dishes.

HOW TO GROW
Cultivate in well-drained – even dry – soil in full sun. Cut back flowered stems, to encourage new leafy growth.

HOW TO HARVEST
Pick fresh leaves as required. Where the plant is evergreen, leaves can be picked in winter as well, but do not remove too much growth as this can weaken the plant.

DOUBLE BONUS
In its native Mediterranean countries winter savory is sometimes called the 'bean herb'. It pairs well with dried bean dishes, and is reputed to reduce any resulting flatulence.

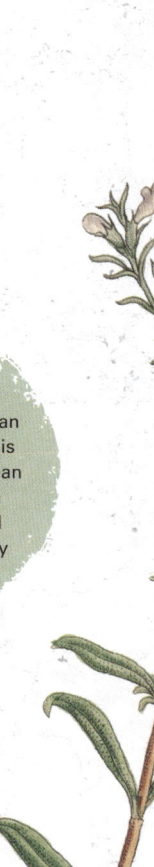

PERENNIAL

Stevia

Stevia rebaudiana aka sugar leaf

As health concerns over refined sugar grow, stevia is fast becoming a 'healthy' alternative sweetener. Its leaves provide a compound, stevioside, that is 300 times sweeter than sucrose: simply chewing a leaf reveals its sweetness.

—

HOW TO USE
Stevia leaves have been used for many years in South America as a sweetener for tea, and they can be combined with other herbs to produce a sweet tea or tisane.

HOW TO GROW
Grow in moist but sandy soil in full sun. Pinch out the tips of young shoots to encourage bushy growth. Cut back flowered stems after flowering.

HOW TO HARVEST
Pick fresh leaves as required.

⚠ Subject to legal restrictions in some countries

Family Asteraceae
Height 20cm/8in
Spread 30cm/12in
Hardiness Zone 6

TOO SWEET
As a calorie-free sweetener, stevia is widely used as an additive in soft drinks and sold under its own name. However, side effects of excessive consumption can include dizziness, headaches, muscle pain and flatulence, so as with all herbs it is best to consume stevia in moderation.

GROWING HERBS

PERENNIAL

Comfrey

Symphytum officinale aka bone set, knit back

Once mulched or steeped in water, this very useful garden plant can provide natural fertilizer for other plants. However, once established, comfrey is difficult to eradicate and can become invasive. A poultice of comfrey leaves was a traditional remedy for fractures and other skin complaints.

⚠ **Foliage can be a skin irritant**

Family Boraginaceae
Height 1.25m/4ft
Spread 60cm/24in
Hardiness Zone 7

HOW TO USE
Leaves can be chopped and applied as a high-nitrogen mulch around the base of other plants or be steeped in a bucket of water to make a liquid fertilizer.

HOW TO GROW
Grow in moist or even wet soil in sun or partial shade. Cut back the dead foliage in autumn or winter.

HOW TO HARVEST
Pick leaves as required to use fresh or to dry.

HAIRY LEAVES
Although the tiny hairs on comfrey leaves can be an irritant to the skin, they dissolve in the mouth so they do not actually feel hairy when young leaves are eaten fresh or cooked (usually as fritters). However, they contain certain alkaloids that have been associated with liver toxicity, so comfrey is best viewed as a curio edible.

TREE

Clove
Syzygium aromaticum

An important spice in international trade, cloves were recorded as being popular across Europe and Asia around 2,000 years ago. Having a clove in the mouth was a means of freshening the breath and also of helping toothache.

Family Myrtaceae
Height 15m/50ft
Spread 4m/13ft
Hardiness Zone 1a

HOW TO USE
Whole cloves are a component of pickling and brining spice mixes. They can also be studded into an orange to make a pomander – a scented winter decoration historically carried to ward off unpleasant odours. Ground cloves are used in baked goods and preserves, particularly mincemeat and gingerbread.

HOW TO GROW
Cultivate in well-drained, fertile soil in full sun. It also can be grown in a large pot as a house plant, if given frost-free conditions and a sunny aspect, although it may not flower. Prune in spring, to keep it to size. Repot annually in fresh compost.

HOW TO HARVEST
Pick the unopened flower buds and dry before storing.

MATURES EARLY
Although they can live for at least a hundred years, a clove tree will be mature (i.e. start flowering and fruiting properly) after only 8–10 years and will reach its full size in 20–30 years.

GROWING HERBS

HERBACEOUS PERENNIAL

Feverfew
Tanacetum parthenium

Historically feverfew was used medicinally for various purposes, although oddly rarely for treating a fever. It is inedible and nor should it be used for home remedies, so its main value is as an ornamental herb. Although a perennial, it is short-lived, but it makes up for this by happily self-sowing around the garden.

⚠ Foliage can be a skin irritant

Family Asteraceae
Height 60cm/24in
Spread 40cm/16in
Hardiness Zone 6

HOW TO USE
As an ornamental plant, feverfew bears daisy-like flowers in profusion in summer. *Tanacetum parthenium* 'Flore Pleno' has double white flowers and makes a good cut flower, while 'Tom Thumb White Stars' is a compact, double-flowered cultivar that is excellent for edging and container planting. The dried leaves can be tied in a sachet of muslin and put with clothes to repel moths.

HOW TO GROW
Feverfew grows best in well-drained, even dry, soil, in full sun. Cut back after flowering, to prevent self-sowing and to stimulate fresh foliage. Remove dead foliage in autumn or late winter.

HOW TO HARVEST
Cut flowers can be gathered as required. Pick leaves for drying in early summer, before flowering.

HEADACHE RESEARCH
In clinical trials feverfew has been shown to be effective in the reduction of migraines, but side effects can be serious and it is contra-indicated in various situations, so seek professional advice before using it.

PROJECT 11

Herb lawns and seats

Camomile lawns have a romantic, country-house feel to them, but they are just as suitable for a small urban plot: they require no mowing, and are a wonderfully fragrant place to lie with a good book on a summer's day. Flowering lawns of other low-growing herbs such as creeping thymes are another no-mow alternative and are great for wildlife. If there is no space for a lawn, create a fragrant seat from a trough or low raised bed. (Sissinghurst garden in Kent has the quintessential example of a camomile seat, as does the Queen's Garden at Kew.)

BASIC PRINCIPLES

The growing depth needs to be at least 20cm/8in, preferably more for seats (make them high enough to sit on comfortably, too). Ensure any container or raised bed has sufficient drainage. The herbs need full sun for the best growth, although will tolerate some dappled shade for part of the day.

HERBS TO USE

Flowering camomile tends to develop straggly growth that leaves gaps in a lawn; for a more compact, non-flowering but still fragrant lawn use *Chamamelum nobile* 'Treneague'. Also ideal are creeping thymes such as *Thymus praecox* subsp. *polytrichus* or *T. serpyllum*.

PLANTING AND MAINTENANCE

Areas to be turned into lawns should be completely weed-free before planting, which saves fiddly digging out of perennial weed roots between the lawn plants later on. Either dig over the area thoroughly, removing all weeds and roots then leaving it for a few weeks to catch any missed bits, or else spray with a proprietary weedkiller composed of glyphosate and wait for the foliage to die completely before digging over to remove all the foliage and roots. Rake the ground thoroughly to level it and remove all surface stones before planting. Herb seats are a much easier to prepare: simply fill the intended container or bed with potting compost.

For both lawns and seats, space plants grown in 9cm/3½in pots 10–15cm/4–6in apart (thus you need around 100 plants per square metre/yard). The closer the plants are placed, the faster the lawn will cover the bare patches, but the more it will cost.

Water the lawn or seat well in the weeks after planting and in dry spells. Do not walk or sit on it for at least three months, to allow the plants a chance to mature and establish themselves; preferably leave it for a full year.

Thereafter, trim the lawn annually with shears to remove any wayward shoots and flowered stems; lightly brush off the clippings.

1. Fill the seat or bench with potting compost to just below the edge.
2. Insert each plant so that the top of the foliage is level with the edge of the seat. then water the plants in well, and keep doing so until well-established.
3. Camomile will form a dense, fragrant mat of foliage.

HERB LAWNS AND SEATS

PERENNIAL

Dandelion

Taraxacum officinale aka lion's teeth, fairy clock, pee the bed

Familiar to all as a difficult weed, dandelions actually have a range of uses for their reputed diuretic and culinary properties. Providing that they are not allowed to set seed, dandelions can therefore easily earn their place in a herb garden.

Family Asteraceae
Height 30cm/12in
Spread 30cm/12in
Hardiness Zone 7

HOW TO USE
Petals can be made into jelly or wine. Leaves can be eaten raw in salads when very young; older ones are best blanched or cooked to remove their bitterness. Leaves and roots are used commercially to flavour drinks (for example, dandelion and burdock), while roots can also be dried and ground to enjoy as a substitute for coffee. Dandelion leaves are also beloved of pets such as guinea pigs and tortoises.

HOW TO GROW
Dandelions grow in most soils, but allow them plenty of depth and an easily workable soil if the roots are to be dug up to use. A position in full sun will promote the best leaf and flower production. Deadhead to ensure plants do not self-sow.

HOW TO HARVEST
Pick flowers and leaves as required. Dig up roots from two-year-old plants in autumn.

CULPEPER ON DANDELIONS AND DOCTORS
After detailing the various medicinal benefits of the dandelion, and how easily it grows ('It flowers in one place or other almost all the year long'), Culpeper takes another opportunity to have a dig at his own (English) profession: 'You see here what virtues this common herb hath, and that is the reason the French and Dutch so often eat them in spring; and now if you look a little further, you may see plainly without a pair of spectacles, that foreign physicians are not so selfish as ours are, but more communicative of the virtues of plants to people.'

SHRUB

Tasmanian mountain pepper
Tasmannia lanceolata aka mountain pepper

Family	Winteraceae
Height	4m/13ft
Spread	2.5m/8ft
Hardiness	Zone 4

Closely related to winter's bark (*Drimys winteri*), a crude cinnamon-type spice, Tasmanian mountain pepper is also known and sold as *Drimys aromatica*. Its dark leaves and reddish stems also have a cinnamon-type scent and it bears white flowers; altogether, it is an attractive, low-maintenance plant.

HOW TO USE
The fresh or dried leaves can be infused to make a tea. Berries are dried and used as a pepper either whole or ground.

HOW TO GROW
Cultivate in a warm, sheltered position in dappled shade and fertile, moist but well-drained soil. This shrub does not need pruning, but can be clipped to keep it in shape (including as a hedge), in spring.

HOW TO HARVEST
Pick leaves as required. Harvest the berries once ripe in autumn; dry them before storing.

ACTIVE INGREDIENT
Chemical compounds in Tasmanian mountain pepper have been found to act against organisms that cause food to go off and also to have antioxidant effects.

TASMANIAN MOUNTAIN PEPPER

PERENNIAL

Thyme
Thymus species

Family	Lamiaceae
Height	20–50cm/8–20in
Spread	20–50cm/8–20in
Hardiness	Zone 5

One of the most versatile culinary herbs, thyme species are many and varied, offering a range of options for a herb garden. Heavy use can result in bare plants (which are best replaced every 3–4 years anyway, as they become woody), so plant several to ensure a ready supply of leaves and flowers.

HOW TO USE
Thyme leaves, both fresh or dried, can be enjoyed as a flavouring in any number of savoury and sweet dishes. They accompany meat and vegetables (especially mushrooms) equally well, and also marry perfectly with chocolate, cream puddings and most fruits, particularly strawberries and peaches. They can be used to infuse marinades, oils and vinegars, too, and are a component herb of both herbes de Provence and bouquet garni. The flowers are edible, with a milder thyme flavour, and can be enjoyed as a garnish or decoration. Commercially, the oil is a component of toothpastes and anti-rheumatism creams.

HOW TO GROW
Well-drained soil in full sun suits all thyme species best. Cut back after flowering, to prevent the plants becoming straggly and to stimulate fresh leaf production.

HOW TO HARVEST
Pick fresh leaves and flowers as required.

> PERENNIAL

NOTABLE SPECIES AND CULTIVARS

T. camphoratus (camphor thyme)
As its name suggests, the leaves have a distinct camphor scent, and they are best reserved for more robust dishes such as roast meats.

T. × *citriodorus* (lemon thyme)
After common thyme, lemon thyme is the species most worth growing for its delicious scent, which goes particularly well with fish dishes and in sweet syrups (for desserts or cocktails). It also makes a good tea, either on its own or mixed with other herbs. A similar plant, *T.* 'Silver Queen', bears silver-and-cream variegated leaves, but is less hardy.

T. 'Fragrantissimus' (orange-scented thyme)
The leaves are scented with orange, and its principal culinary uses are in cocktails and fruit- or cream-based desserts.

T. hyemalis
This species is similar in appearance and uses to common thyme, but it flowers in winter. It is available only in nurseries in France.

PERENNIAL

PERENNIAL

T. praecox subsp. *polytrichus*
A creeping thyme that forms a low mat of furry leaves, which can be used in the kitchen in the same way as other thymes; also makes an excellent lawn or seat, or it can be planted in paving cracks for a fragrant walkway.

T. pulegioides (broad-leaved thyme)
This species has a similar, if slightly less potent, thyme flavour to common thyme, while its glossy, green leaves form a more attractive plant (and are easy to pick from the stalk). A yellow-variegated form of this species is *T. pulegioides* 'Archer's Gold'.

T. serpyllum
Another creeping thyme, very similar in appearance to *T. praecox* subsp. *polytrichus* but with pink flowers. Its essential oils differ and it therefore has more medicinal applications, including as an antiseptic.

T. vulgaris (common thyme)
This most well-known and widely enjoyed culinary thyme also has antiseptic and antifungal properties, and its oil is used in aromatherapy and toiletries. *Thymus vulgaris* 'Erectus' has a more upright form.

ANNUAL

Fenugreek
Trigonella foenum-graecum aka Greek clover

One of the oldest known herbs, fenugreek was cultivated as long ago as 4,000 BC and historically it provided fodder for animals. Its medicinal uses are many and varied, but it is also an important culinary herb. In cool-temperate climates fenugreek can be grown either to its full size or as sprouted seeds or microleaves.

Family Papilionaceae
Height 60cm/24in
Spread 40cm/16in
Hardiness Zone 3

HOW TO USE
Fresh leaves can be added to salads and soups, or cooked in a curry. Seeds (toasted to remove the bitterness) can be added, whole or ground, to pickles, curries (it is an ingredient of curry powder), stews and breads. Fenugreek can also be used as a green manure – a crop that is sown into tired ground, then cut and dug into the soil.

HOW TO GROW
Cultivate in well-drained soil in full sun. Cut back flowering stems to stimulate fresh leafy growth if the seeds are not required. Remove dead plants at the end of the growing season.

HOW TO HARVEST
Pick fresh leaves as required, and harvest seeds once ripe.

LAYERED PLANTING
Broadcast fenugreek seeds on the soil beneath taller vegetable plants such as tomatoes and sweetcorn for a weed-suppressing mat of edible leaves and pretty flowers to attract pollinators.

GROWING HERBS

ANNUAL

Nasturtium

Tropaeolum majus aka garden nasturtium, Indian cress

Often used as a sowing activity for children because of its reliability in germination, the nasturtium is a colourful and useful addition to the garden. The trailing varieties scramble over the ground or most supports or else they hang down from higher containers, but there are also more compact, bushy cultivars available. Flower colour varies from deep purple to cream through the more traditional reds and oranges, but all cultivars can be used in the same way as the true species.

Family Tropaeolaceae
Height 3m/10ft
Spread 2m/7ft
Hardiness Zone 3

HOW TO USE
Fresh leaves can be eaten raw or wilted like spinach: for example, in a risotto. The flowers have a similar peppery flavour to the leaves, and can be added to salads or infused in vinegar. Unripe seeds can be pickled (known as 'poor man's capers'); ripe seeds can be ground as a pepper-like seasoning.

HOW TO GROW
The moister the soil the more vigorous the plant will be, but better leaf production can be at the expense of flowers. Nasturtiums grow in most places, but prefer full sun. They happily self-sow around the garden if flowers and seeds are not harvested. Remove dead plants at the end of the growing season.

HOW TO HARVEST
Pick leaves and flowers as required. Harvest unripe and ripe seeds in summer.

GARDEN SACRIFICE
Growing some nasturtiums in the vegetable patch can attract any aphid infestations to the nasturtiums rather than the vegetable plants.

PROJECT 12

Herbal wreaths

Evergreen herbs last well once cut, and can be chosen to make pretty wreaths for Christmas, Easter or any other time of year. Most wreaths last around two weeks but potentially longer if the driest parts are replaced with fresh growth as needed.

HERBS TO USE

Rosemary, thyme, lavender and bay are all excellent plants for a wreath, either individually or mixed together. Flowering lavender is great for a summer wreath, and rosemary for a fragrant winter one.

Other herbs can be added to the wreath for variety and colour: chillies, sage and oregano, for example. In general, the woodier a plant and the thicker its leaves, the longer it will last once cut. This is also true of different parts of the plant in growth – the older, thicker, darker bay leaves will remain looking good better than thinner, fleshier new growth.

THE WREATH BASE

The base can be made from wire (which is reusable) or twisted compostable hazel (*Corylus*), willow (*Salix*) or dogwood (*Cornus*) stems. There is little need for florists' oasis or sphagnum moss, as the herbs should last well without the need for water.

Circular wreaths are the most basic and easily achievable form to make, but teardrops, ovals or more geometric shapes such as stars can all be achieved relatively simply. Stars are a good candidate for a rosemary decoration.

CREATING THE WREATH

Cut the herbs – using the topmost sprigs of the plant only (it is a good way to use prunings) – into lengths of 10–15cm/4–6in, depending on the size and shape of the wreath.

Bunch together three or four sprigs and wire them on together, wrapping the wire first around the bottom of the sprigs to secure them, then on to the wreath base. Cut off any excess wire and tuck in the end. The next bunch of sprigs should be secured where it overlaps the first by about half its length, and so on until the base is covered. During the making process frequently lift up the wreath as if it was hanging so that any floppy bits can be promptly rectified. The last few bunches need to be tucked under the first to keep the wreath neat.

Once complete, choose the best point from which to hang the wreath – rotate it through a full 360° to confirm this. Then, at the chosen point, attach a loop of wire or string through the plants and on to the base so that the wreath can be hung up.

1. Wire on small bunches (here, of rosemary) at a time, securing firmly them to the base (here of wire).
2. Check that the bunches are evenly spaced around the base.
3. Fruits such as chillies can add colour to the wreath.
4. A wreath is a decorative way to dry and store bay leaves in the kitchen.

HERBAL WREATHS 131

HERBACEOUS PERENNIAL

Nettle
Urtica dioica aka stinging nettle

Although generally considered weeds, nettles can be a boon to the garden and gardener, provided that gloves are worn at all times. The fibrous stems have been used in cloth making, and the plants are invaluable larval food sources for various butterflies.

⚠ **Skin irritant. Potential poison if eaten**

Family Urticaceae

Height 1.5m/5ft

Spread 1m/39in+

Hardiness Zone 7

HOW TO USE
Young fresh leaves can be cooked (never eat them raw) and used in place of spinach in a variety of dishes. The leaves are traditionally used to wrap Cornish Yarg cheese, and can also be a component of beer. The young leaves can be dried to make tea. The plants, once chopped, make an excellent direct mulch or can be added to compost.

HOW TO GROW
Nettles tolerate most soils and positions. Their running roots can quickly become invasive if not controlled by digging out regularly. Cut back flowered stems (provided that they are not covered in caterpillars) for a fresh crop of leaves. Cut back dead stems in winter.

HOW TO HARVEST
Pick fresh young leaves as required. Older leaves have a gritty texture and should be avoided.

GREENER FOOD
Commercially, nettles are grown for their chlorophyll, which is used as a food colouring.

PERENNIAL

Sweet violet

Viola odorata aka violet, viola

Sweet violets were very popular in Victorian England, both to wear as a posy of flowers and as a source of perfume, but their cultivation as a crop dates back to at least 400 BC, in Greece. The species has deep purple flowers – for a white flower plant *V. odorata* 'Alba'.

Family Violaceae
Height 15cm/6in
Spread 50cm/20in
Hardiness Zone 6

HOW TO USE
The young leaves can be added to salads or enjoyed in tea. The flowers can be infused into a sugar syrup, used to make tea or candied for edible cake decorations. They are also pretty as cut flowers. Commercially, sweet violet oil is a component in perfumery and food flavourings Parma violet confectionery is based on the scent of sweet violets.

HOW TO GROW
Sweet violets prefer dappled shade and moist to well-drained soil. They spread and colonize easily. Deadhead regularly, to prolong flowering.

HOW TO HARVEST
Pick flowers and young leaves in spring, as required.

THE VIOLET

The Violet in her greenwood bower,
Where birchen boughs with hazels mingle,
May boast itself the fairest flower,
In glen, or copse, or forest dingle.

This extract from *The Violet* by Sir Walter Scott is both a beautiful celebration of the flower and an indication to the gardener of the plants' preferred habitat.

PERENNIAL

Ginger
Zingiber officinale

Family Zingiberaceae
Height 1.5m/5ft
Spread 1m/39in+
Hardiness Zone 1b

Ginger grows well in a pot, making an attractive house plant for cool-temperate climates, and is a good border plant in hotter areas. A widely used spice, the fresh and dried roots have very different flavours, while stem ginger provides another taste again, but all are known for their reputed ability to stave off nausea.

HOW TO USE
Fresh roots are added to curries, stir-fries, soups, meat and fish dishes and preserves. The root can also be enjoyed (juiced or sliced) in tea, health drinks and cordials. Dried root ginger is crystallized, and balls of stem ginger are candied in syrup. Dried and ground ginger can be put in baking and spicy sauces. The leaves can be wrapped around fish prior to it being steamed or baked, to impart flavour.

HOW TO GROW
Plant fresh rhizomes (roots) in well-drained, rich soil in full sun or partial shade. Ginger needs a highly humid atmosphere. Cut back dead leaves as necessary.

HOW TO HARVEST
Leaves can be cut as needed. Dig up the roots and cut the stem ginger at least eighteen months after planting or once it has reached a usable size; retain some roots for replanting. Freeze or dry roots to preserve them.

SPOT THE DIFFERENCE
Fresh harvests of the rhizomes produce 'stem' ginger, which can be eaten straight away or preserved in sugar syrup. Rhizomes that are allowed to dry become more fibrous and develop a papery skin: called 'root' ginger.

A note on the naming of herbs

Herbs are a wonderful resource for gardeners, but if they are to be used in the kitchen or elsewhere in the home it is essential to ensure the plant has been correctly identified. Common names are given in the herb entries as an identification aid, because they are less bulky to read and also because they are often illuminating (and sometimes amusing) about the herb's historical use. However, these common names can differ widely between countries and even counties or states, with the same common name being applied to many and varied plants. The only name that transcends international borders and is unique to each plant is its botanical Latin name.

Botanical Latin names as applied to flora follow a simple, two-part system: the genus and species name. Thus for *Lavandula angustifolia* (English lavender), *Lavandula* is the genus, encompassing a wide range of other lavender plants with similar characteristics such as *L. stoechas* (French or butterfly lavender); *angustifolia* is the species name, which identifies the plant more closely. Additional parts of the name can include the cultivar ('cultivated variety') or variety name, such as 'Hidcote'; it is placed at the end – *L. angustifolia* 'Hidcote' – and further identifies the plant's characteristics such as its form or colour. Such names can also give clues as to where the plant was bred: 'Hidcote', for example, is a type of English lavender bred at Hidcote gardens.

Plant names are always changing as botanists reclassify plants based on DNA analysis – something not available for the early plant nomenclature experts, who had to rely on a plant's appearance to determine its familial relations. The most up-to-date names may be found by consulting the International Plant Names Index (www.ipni.org). The annually published *RHS Plant Finder* is the best reference for sourcing available garden plants.

Great care has been taken to maintain the accuracy of the information contained in this work. The views expressed in this work are those of the individual authors and do not necessarily reflect those of the publisher or of the Board of Trustees of the Royal Botanic Gardens, Kew. This book is intended as a reference volume only, not as a medical manual. It does not purport to be, nor is it intended to be, a self-treatment guide for the use of medicinal plants. In matters of your health care, we recommend that you consult a qualified health practitioner. The information given here is not intended as a substitute for any treatment that may have been prescribed by your doctor. If you suspect that you have a medical problem, we urge you to seek competent medical help. Neither the publisher nor the authors are engaged in rendering nutritional, medical, or other professional advice or services. The authors, editors and publisher make no representations or warranties with respect to the accuracy, completeness, fitness for a particular purpose or currency of the contents of this book and exclude all liability to the extent permitted by law for any errors or omissions and for any loss damage or expense (whether direct or indirect) suffered by anyone relying on any information contained in this book.

Troubleshooting

Herbs are, of all the garden plants, relatively untroubled by pests and diseases, and major problems are uncommon. The main culprits are listed below. Prevention is always better than cure, so ensure plants are healthy (not wanting for water, nutrients, space or light to grow) by putting them in the optimum position to fight off any potential attacks.

Growing a mosaic of herbs and other types of plants and avoiding the cultivation of large numbers of plants of one type in an area are strategies that reduce the likelihood of significant pest problems. Including long-flowering native plant species (such as borage, marigold, cornflower, sage and mint) in your bed, border or container helps to attract and support beneficial insects. These organisms include pollinators, predators and parasites, which ensure seeds and fruits are set and pest populations are kept to acceptable levels.

PESTS

The worst herb-specific pest is the rosemary beetle, which has very attractive, stripy, iridescent wing casings. Adults and larvae feed on the foliage of many herbs including rosemary, lavender, sage and thyme, but rarely do sufficient damage to kill a plant and are easily dislodged and disposed of by shaking the plant over an upturned umbrella or a sheet.

Aphids tend to focus on soft, new growth and can often be found clustered at stem tips and under leaves, where they drink the sap and excrete sticky 'honeydew' on to the plants (this can then develop a secondary infection of sooty mould). Squashing or cutting off infestations as soon as they are seen helps to prevent their rapid spread.

Mealybugs also feed on sap, but have a fluffy, waxy, white coating and tend to congregate in leaf axils and other less accessible places, making them hard to remove. They prefer warm conditions – indoors in temperate climates – and are best removed individually by hand or with a small paintbrush or cotton bud dipped in soapy water.

Slugs and snails – those perennial feeders on young seedlings and mature plants – can be found in every garden. The most effective defence is early morning or evening patrols in order to dispose of them by hand. Mulching under vulnerable plants, right up to the stem collar, using sharp grit or horticultural sand, can be a helpful way of keeping pesky molluscs at bay – and is especially useful around plants in containers, as it also aids moisture retention.

DISEASES

Plant diseases are fungal, bacterial or viral in origin, with fungal diseases being the most common. Grey mould (*Botrytis* species) can affect any plant in damp, overcrowded conditions, but especially seedlings. Remove affected parts (or the whole plant) as soon as the fluffy, grey fungus is seen, cutting well back into healthy tissue if applicable. Always try to ensure good airflow in and around vulnerable plants.

Mildew is also a fungal disease. Powdery mildew causes a white, powdery coating on the leaves, which is also characterized by leaf wilt or distortion. Downy mildew is less easy to spot, but leaves each have a discoloured blotch on the upper leaf surface with a corresponding mould patch on the underside. Both mildews attack when damp, humid conditions prevail around the leaves, but powdery mildew is able to infect in drier conditions and is usually associated with the plant being repeatedly stressed by underwatering. Remove affected leaves as soon as they are seen, and ensure the plant is adequately watered and mulched.

Mint rust (also fungal) can infect mint, marjoram, oregano and savory plants, causing orange (sometimes yellow and black) pustules on the leaves, which will then brown and die. It also distorts young foliage. Dispose of the whole plant as soon as it is seen. Leek rust has a similar appearance on chives; dispose of the whole plant.

DISORDERS

These are problems that can cause a plant to wilt, distort or discolour but are not caused by pests or pathogens. Under- or overwatering can cause wilting and, in the latter case, root rot. In general, a plant's soil or potting compost should be moist but not wet. Always check the soil before watering because a dry crust can disguise soggy soil beneath and, conversely, a brief rain shower may wet the soil surface but not penetrate the dry soil around the roots.

Yellowing leaves, particularly in potted plants, can be a symptom of a nutrient deficiency such as a lack of nitrogen or magnesium. Failure to flower or fruit can be down to a potassium deficiency. Ensure plants in pots are fed regularly with a balanced fertilizer, and apply a mulch annually to garden beds to maintain a good level of soil nutrients. Poor root development may be an indication of a lack of available phosphorus in the soil or other growing medium. Severe deficiencies are best remedied with the application of liquid fertilizer, as a root drench or foliar feed. Avoid heavy applications of high-nitrogen fertilizers as these can make plant growth overly 'lush' and soft and more prone to sap-feeding insects such as aphids and mealybugs.

DEALING WITH INFESTATION AND INFECTION

Cultivating a biodiverse garden ecosystem full of healthy plants goes a long way towards seeing off any big pest or disease problems. Encourage natural predators of pests – hedgehogs, frogs and toads, birds, beetles, ladybirds and hoverfly larvae will all predate on aphids, slugs and snails. Find the balance between protecting the plants from major damage and ensuring enough food for the predators – and allowing wildlife in general to flourish. There would be no butterflies or moths if gardeners squashed all the caterpillars. Extra help can be enlisted in the form of biological controls – packets of predatory bugs that can be sent through the post to be released on to plants, or nematode solutions that can be watered on to the soil.

Being in the garden regularly and keeping an eye on plants is generally enough to prevent any infestation or infection taking serious hold. However, should something develop, try physical removal of the bugs and affected plant parts first. Chemical controls should be applied only as a last resort. Indeed, there are not many chemical controls now available to the domestic gardener because of the potential damage they do to wildlife; always follow the manufacturer's instructions on application rates and harvest interval periods.

What to do when: Spring

As spring arrives in all its glory, it is a pleasure to get out in the fresh air and sweep away the last vestiges of winter from the garden. Now is a time for creating new life – sowing seed and planting – and for preparing for the season ahead. Any redesigns of the herb garden, or the creation of new ones, is best done now or in autumn.

Initially, only the overwintered herbs will be available to harvest. Some of the earliest herbs to emerge include chives, angelica, fennel, mint, sorrel and lemon balm, but by late spring the whole herb garden is ready for picking.

GROWING
- Sow seed of annual herbs – under cover from early spring onwards or directly outside in late spring (refer to the packet instructions).
- Sow seed of herbaceous perennials and shrubs in the season recommended on the packet. Check on any seeds sown in autumn and left outside for winter.
- As seedlings grow, thin and pot on the strongest, for planting out in late spring and early summer.
- Divide herbaceous perennials and replant or pot up the sections.
- Plant out new herb plants; keep them well-watered until established if the season is dry.

MAINTAINING
- Cut old stems of herbaceous perennials back to the ground.
- Tidy away old growth, leaves and winter debris (and compost it); this will reveal self-sown plants – pot up, transplant or leave *in situ* any that are wanted, such as fennel or borage.
- Weed the ground thoroughly to remove all roots of perennial weeds, and aerate compacted soil with a garden fork.
- Before spreading a layer of mulch over the soil, water the soil thoroughly if it is very dry and, if required, rake in a controlled-release granular fertilizer; take care to prevent the mulch from touching the bases or trunks of plants.
- Water as necessary in dry weather.
- Tidy up pots by weeding and mulching them, replanting pot-bound containers as necessary.
- Feed pots with liquid fertilizer from early spring.
- Remove cloches and other winter protection – in the daytime only at first – once there is minimal risk of frost, and move outside any potted plants that have overwintered indoors, once it is warm enough.

PRUNING
- Cut back hard shrubs such as elder and rosemary in early spring, to control their size, if appropriate.
- Trim shrubs and subshrubs such as bay, sage, thyme and hyssop into a neat shape in mid- or late spring, once all the worst frosts have passed.
- Tie in the new growth of climbers and loosen or replace all old ties.

Summer

Herbs come into their own in summer: their freshest and most luscious growth is in early and midsummer, but they also offer harvests from the whole plant over the growing season when they flower and set seed.

All herbs are available to be gathered in some form over summer. Pick leaves as they are needed and cut bunches for drying (before they flower) to use when fresh foliage is not available. Cut the flowers to eat or for decoration, and harvest the seed for the kitchen or to sow next year.

GROWING
- Plant in the ground or large pots any herbs sown in spring and not already planted out by early summer.
- Continue sowing annuals – directly outside – in early summer and again in later summer for overwintering. Check the packet instructions.
- Take cuttings of perennials and shrubs.

MAINTAINING
- Keep repeat-flowering plants (such as marigolds) going by regular deadheading.
- Cut back herbaceous perennials once they have finished flowering, to stimulate fresh foliage before autumn. Cut back either to the ground (best for chives, for example) or to a lower point on the stem (for mints, lemon balm and the like).
- Continue watering as necessary, particularly pots, and applying a liquid fertilizer to pots every week or two.
- Remove weeds as required, preferably before they are able to flower and set seed.

PRUNING
- Prune shrubs such as lavender and thyme after flowering to prevent them becoming straggly. Cut back to a leaf, removing the flowered part of the stem.
- Trim hedges in midsummer, to maintain their shape.
- Control the spread of mints by cutting off the stolons as they develop over the edges of pots or grow along the ground.

Autumn

As the growing season draws to a close, it is time to preserve the last of the harvests and take stock of the successes and failures of the herb garden. An 'edit' is an invaluable exercise – make notes of potential changes and plants to move, or things to do differently next year. Alternatively, if a redesign or new bed has been planned since summer, now is the time to prepare the soil and plant it.

Many herbs will be producing harvestable seeds and in some cases fruit into autumn, and even annuals such as basil can persist for some time if the first frosts are not too early. However, as the days get colder and darker basil leaves become harder and tougher, so pick any tender ones and use or preserve them in early autumn. Evergreen herbs will persist and tolerate picking into winter.

GROWING
- Dig up a small section of herbs such as mint and chives – including plenty of roots – and pot up for growing indoors, where they can provide fresh leaves throughout winter.
- Sow seed that needs the cold period of winter ('stratification') to germinate, or of any herbs to start growing now for earlier and bigger plants to pot on in spring. Refer to each seed packet for more information.
- Propagate herbs from cuttings if still appropriate.
- Divide herbaceous perennials in early autumn. Replant the sections to increase stock, or pot up to give away.

MAINTAINING
- Ensure new plantings are well-watered until they are established, especially if the season is dry.
- Weed thoroughly.
- Apply a layer of mulch now if it was not added in spring; however, an autumn mulch can be added as well as the spring layer where the soil needs improving.
- Cut back herbaceous perennials where their dead growth is soggy (for example, angelica and lovage); where the stems could cause damage to other plants if they fell (for example, fennel); or where self-sowing is not desired. Other stems can be left – the seed heads can be attractive and provide food and shelter for birds and invertebrates.
- Keep an eye on the garden and remove any stems that do fall on to other plants.
- Move potted plants that need winter protection under cover when frost is forecast, and erect cloches or similar over plants in the ground.

PRUNING
- Tie in any long, waving stems of climbers before winter winds whip and break them.

Winter

Not entirely a time to put one's feet up, winter can still be productive for the herb gardener. Thoughts and sketches of potential new plantings, and browsing of books and catalogues (but keep the size of the garden in mind when ordering!) are worthwhile occupations. Outside, keep an eye on things, in order to prevent any damage.

Apart from overwintered and houseplant herbs, winter harvests are limited to evergreen shrubs such as rosemary and thyme, and hardy plants such as parsley. Do not pick too heavily.

GROWING
- Sow seed of chillies in late winter (following the packet instructions).
- Sow other leafy annuals to harvest as microleaves (see Microleaves, page 16), provided that there is adequate light and some basal heat (from a heated propagator, for example) available.

MAINTAINING
- Keep parsley under protection of a cloche or similar, for better winter harvests.
- Make sure the soil in pots does not dry out completely.
- Check winter protections are still doing their job, particularly in windy weather.
- Cut back any herbaceous perennial stems or other growth that has fallen on to lower plants.
- Brush or shake off heavy snow from the tops of plants, to prevent splitting, and from cloches and fleece coverings, to allow light to penetrate.
- Clean pots and tools ready for the growing season ahead.

Index

A
ache 100
alcohols, infused 40
all good 42
angelica 34
anise 88, 101
anise hyssop 26
aniseed 101
annual herbs 15–17
archangel 34
Asian mint 99
asparagus, Lincolnshire 42
autumn tasks 140

B
baking, herbs for 9–10
basil 90–1
    pesto 94–5
bay 74
bear's chives 31
bee balm 86
beefsteak plant 98
bergamot 86
    citrus 56
biennial herbs 15–17
biting dragon 38
black pepper 102
bladderseed 78
blue sailors 53
bone set 117
borage 43

C
calamint, lesser 57
camomile 52
caraway 51
cardamom 66
Carolina allspice 46
celery leaf 36
chervil 35
    sweet 88
chicory 53
chilli oil 40
chilli pepper 47–50
Chinese chives 30

Chinese parsley 58
chives 27
    Chinese 30
    garlic 30
cilantro 58
citrus bergamot 56
clove 118
clover, Greek 128
cocktails, herbs for 104–5
comfrey 117
containers 19–20
cooking, herbs for 9
cool tankard 43
coriander 58
    Vietnamese 99
corn poppy 96
cress
    Indian 129
    Pará 25
crocus, saffron 59
cumin 62
cut flowers, herbs as 10, 54–5

D
daisy, electric 25
dandelion 122
designing with herbs 16–19
devil-and-back-ten-times 100
dill 33
diseases 136–7
disorders 137
drinks, herbs for 10
drying herbs 76–7

E
easy-care herbs 10–11
edging 18–19
elder 112
elderflower 112
electric daisy 25
English lavender 75
English mace 24
epazote 65
equipment 11

F
fairy clock 122
fat hen 42
fennel 68–70
fenugreek 128
feverfew 119
field poppy 96
flossflower 24
French tarragon 38

G
garden myrrh 88
garlic
    bear's 31
    chives 30
    wild 30
ginger 134
good King Henry 42
Greek clover 128
green roof, herbs as a 84–5

H
hardiness zones 8–9
haridra 63
harvesting seed 68–9
herb fennel 70
holy ghost 34
hop 72
horseradish 37
hyssop 73
    anise 26

I
ice cubes 105
Indian cress 129
indoors, growing herbs 20–1
invasive herbs 19

J
jatiphala 87

K
knit back 117

L
Latin names 135
laurel, bay 74
lavender, English 75
lawns, herb 120–1
lemon balm 79
lemon verbena 32
lemongrass 64
Lincolnshire asparagus 42
lion's teeth 122
lovage 78
love parsley 78

M
mace 87
    English 24
marigold 45
marjoram 92
maudlin 24
Mexican tea 65
milfoil, sweet 24
mint 80–3
    Asian 99
monarda 86
mountain pepper 123
mountain spinach 39
mustard 44
myrrh, garden 88
myrtle 89

N
naming of herbs 135
nasturtium 129
nettle 132
nutmeg 87

O
oils 40–1
orach 39
oregano 93

P
Pará cress 25
parsley 100
    Chinese 58

love 78
paths 18–19
pee the bed 122
pelargonium, scented 97
pepper 102
    Tasmanian mountain 123
pepper root 37
perennial herbs 12–13
pesto 94–5
pests 136, 137
planting out herbs 16–18
pollen, harvesting fennel 68–9
poppy 96
pot marigold 45

R
ramsoms 31
rau ram 99
Roman camomile 52
roof, green 84–5
rose 103
rosemary 109

S
saffron 59
sage 107–8
salad burnet 113
savory
    summer 114
    winter 115
scented waters 40
seats, herb 120–1
seed
    buying 15
    harvesting 68–9
    sowing 16
shiso 98
shrubs 13–14
soil conditions 11–12
sorrel 106
sowing seeds 16
spicebush 46
spinach, mountain 39
spirits 40–1
spring tasks 138

St Michael's flower 34
starflower 43
stevia 116
stinging nettle 132
succory 53
sugar leaf 116
summer savory 114
summer tasks 139
sweet basil 90–1
sweet chervil 88
sweet Cicely 88
sweet marjoram 92
sweet Nancy 24
sweet shrub 46
sweet violet 133
sweet woodruff 71

T
tarragon, French 38
Tasmanian mountain pepper 123
thyme 124–7
tisanes 60–1
toothache plant 25
topiary herbs 110–11
trees 13–14
turmeric 63

V
vertical herb garden 28–9
Vietnamese coriander 99
vinegars 40–1
viola 133
violet, sweet 133

W
wasabi 67
waters, scented 40–1
wildlife, herbs for 10
winter savory 115
winter tasks 141
witloof 53
woodruff, sweet 71
wormseed 65
wreaths, herbal 130–1

Brimming with creative inspiration, how-to projects and useful information to enrich your everyday life, Quarto Knows is a favourite destination for those pursuing their interests and passions. Visit our site and dig deeper with our books into your area of interest: Quarto Creates, Quarto Cooks, Quarto Homes, Quarto Lives, Quarto Drives, Quarto Explores, Quarto Gifts, or Quarto Kids.

First published in 2019 by White Lion Publishing, an imprint of The Quarto Group.
The Old Brewery, 6 Blundell Street
London, N7 9BH,
United Kingdom
T (0)20 7700 6700 F (0)20 7700 8066
www.QuartoKnows.com

Text © 2019 Holly Farrell
Project photographs © 2019 Jason Ingram
Illustrations © the Board of Trustees of the Royal Botanic Gardens, Kew, unless otherwise stated

All rights reserved. No part of this book may be reproduced or utilized in any form or by any means, electronic or mechanical, including photocopying, recording or by any information storage and retrieval system, without permission in writing from White Lion Publishing.

A catalogue record for this book is available from the British Library.

ISBN 978-0-7112-3936-4

10 9 8 7 6 5 4 3 2 1

Typeset in Stempel Garamond and Univers
Design by Arianna Osti
Art Director Glenn Howard

Printed in China

Picture acknowledgements
t=top; b=below; m=middle; l=left; r=right

© Alamy: 24l Gary K Smith, 121b John Glover

© GAP Photos: 13l Friedrich Strauss, 15r Elke Borkowski, 85 Hanneke Reijbroek

© Jason Ingram: 2, 6–7, 29, 41, 55al+r, 55ml, 55bl+r, 61, 69, 74l, 77, 84, 94l, 95l, 105, 111, 121al+r, 131,

© Shutterstock: 9 Jayne Newsome, 10 CTatiana, 11l Piccia Neri, 11r Lauren Maki, 12 Franz Peter Rudolf, 13r sanddebeautheil, 14 Maren Winter, 15l Alexander Raths, 16 Kayla Waldorff, 17l Peter Turner Photography, 17r Kayla Waldorff, 18 Del Boy, 19l Peter Turner Photography, 19r rustamank, 20 Diana Taliun, 21l Hannamariah, 21r ioks, 22–3 Drozdowski, 26l JurateBuiviene, 31l Ivan Marjanovic, 33l Nine Johnson, 34b blacograf, 36l guentermanaus, 39l greenair, 43l F.Neidl, 49b YukoF, 51l tim_zml, 52l areeya_ann, 55mr Svetlana Lukienko, 57l FMB, 59l barmalini, 64 sarocha wangdee, 67l Piti Tan, 67r jopelka, 70l mirzamlk, 71l Bildagentur Zoonar GmbH, 73l BelkaG, 78l beta7, 81l kridsada tipchot, 86l Vahan Abrahamyan, 89l Katinkah, 91l Olexandr Panchenko, 93l Madeleine Steinbach, 96l Katarzyna Golembowska, 99l wasanajai, 99r Puttida Channum, 101l Mahathir Mohd Yasin, 102l Marshmallowz, 106l alexmak7, 108l Yolanta, 114l Ed Samuel, 115l ChWeiss, 116l HandmadePictures, 119l angelakatharina, 123l Juraj Kovac, 125l Branimir Dobes, 126 Katarzyna Mazurowska, 127a JurateBuiviene, 128l Madeleine Steinbach, 132l Dazajny, 134l wavebreakmedia, 135 JSOBHATIS16899, 136 svetkor, 138 paula french, 140 gorillaimages, 141 Eris and Edrington Co

The publishers wish to thank Martyn Rix and the Kew Library Art and Archives team, and Tony Hall, Melanie-Jayne Howes and Richard Wilford.